Captain of the Andes

The Life of José
de San Martín,
Liberator
of Argentina,
Chile and Peru

MARGARET H. HARRISON

COSIMOCLASSICS

NEW YORK

Captain of the Andes:
The Life of José de San Martín, Liberator of Argentina, Chile and Peru
Cover Copyright © 2009 by Cosimo, Inc.

Captain of the Andes: The Life of José de San Martín, Liberator of Argentina, Chile and Peru
was originally published in 1943.

For information, address:
P.O. Box 416, Old Chelsea Station
New York, NY 10011

or visit our website at:
www.cosimobooks.com

Ordering Information:
Cosimo publications are available at online bookstores. They may
also be purchased for educational, business or promotional use:
- *Bulk orders:* special discounts are available on bulk orders for reading
groups, organizations, businesses, and others. For details contact
Cosimo Special Sales at the address above or at info@cosimobooks.com.
- *Custom-label orders:* we can prepare selected books with your cover or
logo of choice. For more information, please contact Cosimo at
info@cosimobooks.com.

Cover Design by www.popshopstudio.com

ISBN: 978-1-60520-913-5

San Martín was convinced that the enthusiasm
for independence in Lima was purely emotional and transient;
and to instill a deeper understanding of his vision and to create
permanent co-operation he organized the Order of the Sun.
Of all countries on the South American continent, Peru's population
was least fitted for popular government, and he hoped through
this new order to transform their sense of aristocratic tradition
into pride in the achievement of their independence. The Order
was to be a group of distinguished patriots and deserving men.

—from Chapter XV: "Dark Days in Lima"

THE VISION OF SAN MARTIN

*To understanding friendship between Argentina
and the United States, based on mutual appreciation
of the men who shaped their destinies.*

PREFACE

IN THE Club del Progreso of Buenos Aires, Argentina, hangs the curious and unforgettable painting which is reproduced as the frontispiece of this volume. It shows an old man seated at a table; he has thrust aside a pile of documents and a heavy inkstand, and he sits deep in thought. His magnificent eyes are shaded by his hand; there is a singular nobility about his tragic face. The canvas depicts skilfully the medley of past events surging in his memory—old battles, with soldiers doggedly holding their ground under their commander's eye, horses plunging forward, hoarse cries of wounded men; white giant cordilleras and soldiers sick with fatigue, gasping in the thin air but following their leader blindly on and up narrow, treacherous paths, over slippery rocks towards the summit, red with the new dawn; a victorious general proudly unfurling a new flag to a newly freed people. Last of all, in quiet contrast to these martial pictures, is a burning memory of two earnest men, alone in a council chamber, discussing the fate of a continent.

The title of this painting is "The Vision of San Martín." The old man is Don José de San Martín. His genius gave three countries their freedom, yet he died poor and forgotten in a small French town.

Storms of intrigue and slander roared around this man, but time dims factional passions, and in his native Argentina he is honored today as first among his country's heroes. Children are taught to revere him as the Father of the Republic. A most idealistic devotion is given to the "Saint of the Sword"; all classes know of his lonely, austere life, dedicated utterly to an ideal of American independence to which he sacrificed love, family happiness and personal ambition, and for which he silently endured years of malicious persecution. Today in the Cathedral of Buenos Aires a soldier in the destiny-making uniform of San Martín's Grenadiers stands constantly at attention before the bronze and marble tomb of this Conqueror of the Andes. At the foot of the mausoleum are three symbolic figures representing Argentina, Chile, and Peru mourning their champion.

San Martín's life was mysterious, full of change and tragedy. He once said, "My youth belonged to Spain, my middle life to Argentina, my old age to myself." Because of his intense reserve, he remains one of history's most enigmatic personalities, and the two stupendous renunciations of his life have been continually misunderstood. What kind of man was this who threw away an ultra-brilliant career won by twenty years of distinguished service in the Spanish army, fighting and defeating Napoleon's best generals, in order to set out for a far-off country where he was absolutely unknown? Then when he had changed the future of a continent by his spectacular triumphs, why did he turn again to Europe, abandoning his honors for a life of exile? What were his motives? And as the Conqueror of the Andes sat in a humble Boulogne lodging, old and blind, and with only his daughter to watch over him, could he be sure that he had been true to his life's ideal? He was an unusual man, and his is an unusual story.

Margaret H. Harrison.

San Francisco,
California.
January, 1943.

CONTENTS

ILLUSTRATIONS

Captain of the Andes

PAMPA INDIANS

Chapter I

CHILDHOOD IN ARGENTINA

JOSÉ FRANCISCO DE SAN MARTÍN was born on February 25, 1778, in the Department of Yapeyú, in what is now Argentina. Yapeyú, on the right bank of the Uruguay River, was the site of one of the old Jesuit missions to the Guarani Indians. José was the son of Juan de San Martín, at that time administrator of the Department, and a native of old Castile. Juan de San Martín had come to America in 1765, after serving seventeen years in the Spanish army. He first was employed drilling troops in Buenos Aires. Later, during the turbulent times in Argentina that followed the expulsion of the Jesuits in 1768, Juan had been employed by the government at Buenos Aires as administrator of the enormous hacienda of Las Caleras de las Vacas, formerly a Jesuit property. He seems to have been, if not a brilliant man, at least a very careful, practical person, bending all his energies to the accomplishment of every task; he dreamed no visions, but he was the very soul of kindliness and honor.

His wife had more adventurous blood. She also came from old Castile, of an ancient noble family which long before her birth had been reduced to respectable poverty. Years afterwards one of her sons, Justo Rufino, applied for admission to a crack Argentine regiment for which proof of the blue blood of the applicant was necessary. He produced a statement, made under oath by the mayor of his mother's village, that Gregoria Matorras, all her ancestors and descendants were Christians "free from evil race strains of the Moor, the heretic or of any Jew recently converted to our holy Catholic Church; and neither have they even been in trouble with the Holy Office of the Inquisition." In short, a cleancut family record!

Gregoria was a gallant soul, this daughter of "poor and honorable hidalgos." Still extant is the petition, dated 1767, in which she asks permission of the King of Spain to go to South America, accompanied by her cousin Jerónimo. The reason for her going is unknown. She was only twenty-six, and it was a daring undertaking for any young woman. Three years after her arrival she married Don Juan; her cousin became a famous explorer and, later, Governor of Tucumán.

In 1774 Don Juan took up his post as administrator of the Department of Yapeyú. The Jesuit missions, among which Yapeyú was one of the most flourishing, had been thirty in number and lay along the banks of the Uruguay and Parana rivers. After the expulsion of the Jesuits in 1768, the missions were secularized and finally placed under a single political and military administration.

The South American scene was changing far more than Don Juan or Doña Gregoria realized; they had little sense of anything unstable in remote and idyllic Yapeyú, which had prospered since its founding by the Society of Jesus in 1626. The Guarani Indians were gentle and friendly and had been well trained by the missionaries. Too little time had elapsed since their teachers' expulsion to undo the effects of discipline and regular life. Even in 1778 the

2

settlement was noted for its wealth in cattle. The Jesuits had cultivated farms, orchards and gardens in a wilderness. There was a herbarium of four thousand plants; roses and jasmine, and orange, lemon, fig, peach, apple and pear trees abounded. Palm trees, algarrobas and gigantic ferns marked the beginnings of the jungles which encroached towards the north. The home of the San Martíns was in the ancient Jesuit college, and on all sides were vast storehouses of food.

Here the five children born to the young couple spent their earliest youth. Their names were Manuel Tadeo, Juan Fermin, Justo Rufino, José Francisco, and a daughter Maria Elena, who survived them all. There was much to interest the children in this exotic spot. The sun was always shining, the air was heavily fragrant, and the colors of tropical flowers dazzled the eye. They played with the young Guarani Indians in the fruit orchards, wandered along the banks of the great river, chased butterflies and listened to the strange cries of wild birds. So keen was the impression of romance and beauty created in the mind of little José that, after an absence of twenty-seven years he still carried a sense of pride that he had been born in America. There was another side to the life: the peril of Portuguese and hostile Indian raids was a black shadow over Yapeyú. The territory of the missions was kept in constant anxiety because of the always latent hostility between Spanish and Portuguese, for the Portuguese kept an ever-threatening eye on the lands washed by the Uruguay. In later years, José de San Martín, when he was overfatigued and nervously exhausted, suffered from nightmares of a surprise attack by Indians. At one time

3

his father petitioned the Viceroy to send him enough troops to conduct a decisive campaign against these enemies, but was told that the state of the treasury did not warrant the expense. There was nothing to be done, therefore, but maintain strict vigilance and hold the post.

Despite the infinite possibilities of graft offered by his position at a time when corruption in office was the accepted thing, Don Juan lived frugally on his scant salary and he and Gregoria made anxious plans for the children's future. There is a testimonial from Yapeyú's leading settlers praising his conscientious qualities as administrator, and the impartiality and justice of his management. "He has always seen to our affairs," reads the paper, "with love and with charity." In 1781 the family left Yapeyú for Buenos Aires when Don Juan was suddenly transferred there. The reason for the transfer is obscure; perhaps he was the victim of a political intrigue. At any rate the family never returned to their Indian paradise.

To the children brought up in Yapeyú's Arcadian simplicity, great Buenos Aires, with its thousands of people, must have seemed bewildering. Since 1776 Buenos Aires had been the capital of the newly created Viceroyalty of La Plata, which stretched from the mouth of the La Plata River almost to the Pacific Ocean and comprised the modern states of Argentina, Paraguay, Uruguay and Bolivia.

Little Don José was sent to learn his letters at a primary school in Buenos Aires. Of his early school days, one or two tales are revealing. Don Juan Gutiérrez heard an ancient, who had once sat on the class benches, say that

4

José de San Martín was the outstanding personality of the school. "Even if he had accomplished nothing, I should never have forgotten him." Sarmiento, Argentina's greatest statesman, writes that San Martín is supposed to have divided the boys into two bands, Guarani Indians and Portuguese soldiers, who engaged in wild combat on the school grounds. At the mature age of seven, the Conqueror of the Andes was already a fighter.

Still greater changes soon came to the San Martín family. By an order of King Charles III, dated May 21, 1785, Captain San Martín was transferred to Spain. He sailed for Cadiz with his Gregoria, his children and his small store of household goods on the frigate "Santa Balbina." Of all the family group, José was the only one who ever returned to the new world.

From Cadiz poor Captain Juan set out for Madrid in an effort to obtain a position that would enable him to give his children an education. On the strength of his honorable record he petitioned the crown to be advanced to the rank of lieutenant colonel and returned to service in America.

Barring that of merit, there was no reason why he should succeed in his quest. He was fifty-seven years old, broken in health, and he had no friends to speak for him at court. Discouraged after months of waiting for a reply which never came, he asked to be assigned to Malaga, and this petition was granted. Realizing that his own professional career was over, he felt that the best he could do for his boys was to place them in active military life.

When he died in 1796, Juan de San Martín had the satisfaction of knowing that all of them, youngsters though they were, were seeing service under the banners of Spain, and all were distinguishing themselves. That was happiness enough for the simple gentleman whose loyalty to his king had been his life's ideal.

Chapter II

EIGHTEENTH CENTURY COLONIAL SPAIN

THE LAST QUARTER of the eighteenth century—the years of José de San Martín's childhood and early manhood—found the unwieldy colonial empire of Spain cracking; forces that had gone beyond control were slowly rotting it away. It must always be remembered that Spanish America's revolt against Spain was in no sense a revolt of the masses, but a break instigated by the aristocratic Creoles or Spanish-descended native-born whites, whose lack of any future rendered them desperate.

The whites were in the majority in Argentina, Uruguay, Chile and Southern Brazil. Indians were the predominant race in the sections along the Andes from Bolivia and Peru northwards, as well as in Paraguay, parts of Venezuela, Mexico and throughout Central America. The very few negroes in Argentina were almost exterminated in the Wars of Independence, but negroes predominated northward along the Atlantic Coast and the shores of the Caribbean. Alliances between blacks and whites were common, and a wide social gulf separated the unmixed Spanish race from the people of mixed blood—mestizos, mulattoes and zambos, the latter being the product of unions between negroes and Indians.

The root of endless trouble lay in the contempt felt by the Spaniard from Spain towards the Creole or Spaniard

7

born in America. The Spaniard's attitude is best expressed by a certain judge, Aguirre by name, who went to Mexico in the seventeenth century. "As long as there remains in La Mancha a shoemaker of Castile with a mule, that cobbler would have the right to govern South America before a native." The Creoles, being considered inferior beings, were almost entirely shut out from affairs of state, and this line was drawn even among the clergy. Thus of the one hundred seventy Viceroys, only four were American-born; and of the six hundred captains general and governors in the new world, only fourteen were Creoles. The doors were closed to high military, political and ecclesiastical appointment.

It was the custom of wealthy Creoles to send their sons to Europe to be educated, but these youths returned home with no opportunity to make use of their training. Instead of being allowed to give intelligent assistance to the government, they were ignored; the result was that they formed an unassimilated, discontented group, given either to dissipation or intrigue. Supersensitive because they were held inferior, they offered an ever-fertile field for revolution.

They were constantly irritated by the arrogance of their Spanish masters. Spanish residents would often solicit husbands among their own countrymen, preferring Spaniards without fortune or business to Creoles possessed of both. Spaniards even went as far as to say that they would love their children more had they been born in Europe, and a European son was held in higher esteem than a native of America. There was no way to argue against this blind prejudice. It was the myth not only of the blood but of

8

MILK BOYS

the soil; but it was also a fact of existence, as is the Aryan myth in National Socialism today.

The Spaniard from Spain never looked on the new world as his home. If he were in secular life, he had emigrated in the spirit of high adventure, hoping to extract gold from that exciting region and return to settle comfortably by his hearth when his fighting days were over. The accepted Spanish code of the sixteenth century was rugged individualism, and a Spanish gentleman worthy of his heritage would have scorned to spend his vigorous years in idle luxury. Later, it was a different story when Peru's fabulous treasures had wrought their subtle corruption and the race, grown soft, prized the ease and safety that have ruined too-successful nations since the world began.

As it was very difficult for Spanish women to obtain permission to emigrate, the mestizo class, of mixed Spanish and Indian blood, rapidly increased and naturally looked to the Creoles for leadership. When the time came, the mestizos formed the backbone of the patriotic armies in the War of Liberation. In the eighteenth century, however, the great mass of people in the colonies were as loyal to Spain as ever. They led a simple agricultural life, cultivating fruit and vegetables, tending herds of cattle. The large estates were self-sufficient, and the general attitude towards the masters was the trusting one of obedient children.

Captain Basil Hall, arriving in Chile during the War of Independence, was impressed by the fact that the mixed races spoke with so little vindictiveness of their enemies the Spaniards, while the prosperous classes "never allowed themselves to think of their ancient rulers without expressing the bitterest animosity." The Creoles had nothing to lose and everything to gain in their struggle against Spain, but the peasant's position was not materially changed by the defeat of the Spanish authority. The latter merely substituted one master for another, but the Creole obtained political independence, security of person and property, and increased prosperity through the lifting of the cruel trade restrictions imposed by Spanish rule.

These trade restrictions rendered the Creole's future perfectly hopeless. As owners of plantations and estancias, they naturally were ambitious to employ their wealth in active commerce, but they were forbidden on pain of death to trade with foreigners, and no stranger was allowed to visit the country. No ship of any nation save Spain was allowed to enter a South American port. Needless to say, as time went on, smuggling flourished, and the laws were constantly evaded even at tremendous risks. In 1678, the Portuguese, always hostile, established a fortified port, Colonia del Sacramento, across the estuary from Buenos Aires, and this became the notorious centre of both the Portuguese and the English contraband trade.

Any form of agriculture which might interfere with production in the mother country was forbidden. The cultivation of flax, hemp and saffron was banned. When the Cadiz merchants complained of the falling off of their wine sales, there came an order to uproot all vines flourishing in American provinces. Special permission was given Buenos Aires to cultivate grapes and olives in sufficient quantity for the table, but the culture of the grape and

10

olive for the market was generally forbidden as it competed with two of Spain's leading industries.

Peru was always, because of its precious metals, the favorite of the Spanish crown. She profited especially by the system of trade fleets from Spain—merchant ships protected against pirates by an escort of galleons. Two such fleets arrived annually in the new world. One put in at Vera Cruz, after stopping at Havana; the other anchored first at Cartagena and then continued to Porto Bello on the Isthmus of Panama. There, for six weeks, a great fair was held to sell the cargoes of the trade fleet. The seamen, exhausted after their long journey, had to unload the cargoes in the tropical heat, under frightful sanitary conditions. The galleons usually departed after burying sometimes half—but always a third—of the crew, but that was unimportant to the Spanish exporters, to whom the fairs brought profits of from one to three hundred percent.

As the River Plate country (central Atlantic coast) was forbidden to trade directly with Spain, European goods consigned to Buenos Aires (chief city of the River Plate area) had to be sent to the Isthmus of Panama, shipped to Peru, on the west coast, then transported over the Andes. On their arrival at Buenos Aires, articles often sold at six times the original cost. It took five hundred Argentine cattle to pay for one fine imported coat. The Porteños, as Buenos Aires inhabitants were called, could rarely pay the exorbitant prices of the goods imported via Peru. Theirs was a hard struggle. In the seventeenth century a five-year-old suit of clothes was considered fairly smart in Argentina. Gradually the Portuguese contraband nest across the river drummed up a thriving business and goods from England were sold over the Brazilian border at reduced prices. Greatly would the Porteños of that day have wondered at the story of a modern immigrant wife who picked up a silver coin in the streets of Buenos Aires.

"Drop the trash," cried her husband. "We came to Argentina for gold, not worthless silver."

Considering the long-continued and relentless discrimination, it is a wonder the colonies protested so little. Taxes and duties were always oppressive. Tobacco, salt, gunpowder, and quicksilver were closed royal monopolies; the resultant exorbitant cost left the people without an adequate supply. The *alcabala,* a tax levied on every transfer of goods, affected all classes. Except for a few small mutinies, all this oppression was suffered patiently for over two centuries. Now and then came a respectful complaint to the crown from his majesty's loyal subjects overseas. That was all. The theory that Spanish colonial dominions were subject directly to the crown remained unchallenged. The link was with the king, not with the Spanish nation, the lands being held in fief by the crown through a grant from the pope. The affairs of the colonies were regulated by the king, assisted by the Council of the Indies, governing by a separate code of laws, namely, the laws of the Indies. For two hundred years the results of decisions under this code were endured by the colonists with the same resignation with which they bore nature's cataclysms, earthquakes and raging hurricanes.

At the time (1774) when Don Juan and Doña Gregoria

de San Martín went out to Yapeyú, Argentine conditions were slowly changing for the better. The fair of Porto Bello had been abolished in 1740, but trade from Buenos Aires overland to Peru was still forbidden. Alarmed at the increase of illegal traffic, the Spanish government at last realized something must be done. The advantage which smuggling enjoyed over legitimate trade was destroying morale; disrespect for law was rampant.

Accordingly, when Charles III became King of Spain in 1759, the harsh trade laws were mitigated. Due to conflict with the Portuguese, Buenos Aires was growing politically important. After 1767 a ship carrying mail and merchandise ran between Spain and the River Plate every three months, later every two months. In 1776, Buenos Aires was permitted to trade with the other Spanish colonies in America, except that overland traffic with Peru was still forbidden. Finally even this restriction was removed; in 1778, Buenos Aires was open to commerce with all parts of the Spanish empire. She had come into her own in 1776 when the Viceroyalty of La Plata was formed; this comprised Argentina, Uruguay, Paraguay and that part of Peru known as Alto Peru, now the country of Bolivia.

The reforms had come too late. The general alleviation of conditions did not kill the germs of discontent among the Creoles, whose political future still remained restricted. The success of the North American revolution against Great Britain thrilled them profoundly. At great risk, for their introduction into the country was forbidden, medals bearing the motto *"Libertas Americana"* were circulated. As one writer says, "With the medals, circulated the new ideas—they could not be arrested."

13

The world was in one of its periodic swings towards liberalism, and the revolution in France was breaking on a horrified Europe. Wealthy Creoles who had traveled or studied abroad passed their time feverishly absorbing the principles of free thought and individual freedom which were setting the outside world on fire. Ironically, the Spanish government, unconscious of the abyss yawning ahead of it, joined its ally France in blessing the cause of the North American revolutionists.

In Buenos Aires all was outwardly quiet. The eighteenth century had witnessed only small outbreaks against local injustices, the most important being the revolt of the Comuneros in Paraguay. In 1780 came the Chilean rebellion of the three Antonios—Berney, Gramuset and Rojas—which declared the office of Captain-General of Chile independent of Spain. The revolt was suppressed, and for some strange reason the three Antonios were given their lives, but deported. The revolt of Tupac Amaru in Peru, that same year, had a more horrible ending. A descendant of the Incas, Tupac Amaru gathered an army of Indians and besieged Cuzco, but was finally captured. In May, 1781, he was executed with frightful tortures in the public square of Lima, thus furnishing the native mind with a gruesome example of the fate of all who questioned almighty Spain.

Thus the eighteenth century in the colonies slipped by quietly. The Viceroy's Court in Buenos Aires dreamed through pleasant, carefree days. The Creoles plotted a little, and whispered much dangerous talk among themselves. The mestizos and mulattoes plodded amicably about their business. The stage was set, the background prepared, but the actors had not yet taken their places. The chief actor, José de San Martín, was as yet a schoolboy in Madrid.

Chapter III

A CREOLE SCHOOLBOY IN MADRID

AFTER an absence of more than twenty years in the new world, Captain Juan de San Martín brought his family back to Spain—a Spain far different from the one he had left. Although few realized it, her glory was tarnished and shopworn. Governed by Charles III, who was too much of a Bourbon and a Frenchman to sense the temper of the nation, the Spaniards found their accustomed social activities hampered in every direction by blue laws which infuriated them. Naturally, he rapidly became the most unpopular of monarchs.

Charles III has been called "the only good, great and patriotic King that Providence had vouchsafed to Spain in modern times." This is exaggeration. He was good, but certainly not great nor, from the Spanish point of view, was he patriotic. In his life of Goya, Charles Poore makes a shrewder analysis. "This was the best of the Spanish Bourbons. Accustomed to the family's galloping incompetence, one is more ready to see the good in Charles III's pedestrian excellences." Charles was a worthy soul and meant well. His reforms were excellent, but he had no tact, and he completely failed to understand Spanish tradition, so in his subjects' eyes, he remained a meddling, interfering foreigner.

He made himself characteristically hated because of

16

CHARLES III OF SPAIN
BEST OF THE BOURBONS

laws forbidding the wearing of broadbrimmed hats and the long cloaks that went with them, as such costumes served as easy disguises and encouraged rioting. Charles favored the three-cornered hat of Paris as a substitute, but it failed to go over. He disapproved of dancing and the theatre and, worst of all, he abolished bullfighting.

Under Count Aranda, the king's minister, sweeping social reforms were instituted, agriculture was improved, roads and canals were constructed, hospitals and free schools established. The government subsidized factories and brought experts from abroad to teach new methods. Streets were lighted at night, drainage was looked after and life was safer than it had ever been. It was all in vain. Spain, scrubbed and made to mind, was in the grip of a benevolent despotism, which it mocked, jibed and writhed under.

To make matters worse, Charles' brief venture into foreign politics proved disastrous. In March, 1778, the French government recognized the new republic of the United States; as a result, war was declared between Great Britain and France. In June, 1779, Spain entered the war against the British, and fighting broke out in all parts of the world. The result of this war was a fearful blow to Spain's prestige, for the peace terms forced her to sign away Gibraltar.

This summary indicates briefly the changed and changing conditions into which Captain San Martín brought his family. What to do with his four sons, to assure them the best future? He soon found that if one were ambitious for a career of distinction, the thing to do was to join the army, then being organized after the Prussian model of Frederick the Great. So the three older San Martín boys were entered in the *Compañia Americana,* in which many colonials were serving. José, the youngest, was placed in a seminary of nobles founded by Philip V in 1727. The school stood in the Calle de la Princesa, near the Duke of Alba's palace in Madrid. Originally open only to those of the *sangre azul,* the seminary now admitted commoners at the discretion of the directors, and in the San Martín case, the directors seemed impressed not only by the father's honorable record but by his intense ambition for his solemn-faced little boy.

José had good reason for feeling solemn. The school's aristocratic and stiffly formal atmosphere was a strain for the child newly come from his Indian playmates in the wilds of Yapeyú and his very brief schooling in colonial Buenos Aires. In Madrid he was placed in competition with the sons of Castilian grandees, who, if not noted for their application, had received far better training, came from luxurious homes and considered themselves the Lord's anointed. José was the Creole son of a penniless captain set down in the most snobbish environment of Europe. One can imagine the sarcastic treatment, the daily snubs he had to endure, the hundred subtle ways in which he was made to feel he was not of the elect. The glory and arrogance that was Castile and the utter insignificance of Argentina to the glamorous circle—these things were indelibly impressed on his young mind.

Shy and extremely reserved, José went methodically about his tasks and developed superb self-control. His mind was exact, best in science and mathematics; he was singularly lacking in literary talent. His only aesthetic

18

interest was water-color painting, preferably marine scenes. He acquired a fair knowledge of French, and later this language opened to him the enlightened thought of the Encyclopedists. San Martín left no accounts of his school days, and never referred to them in after years.

He left the seminary in 1789, after four years, because his family could no longer afford to keep him there. His brothers were now in active service in the Regiment of Soria, and he, too, must be about the business of life. In July of 1789, therefore, this child of eleven, at an age when the pupil of today is completing grammar school, was granted permission to enter the Regiment of Murcia, then stationed in Malaga. He knew nothing of the world; his studies had been too brief for any culture; of military science, he was completely ignorant. The ranger camp, the noisy garrison, the bloody battlefield—these were to be his training schools. They hardened the timid boy into the austere and experienced soldier, tough and resourceful.

Chapter IV

A SOLDIER OF SPAIN

JOSÉ DE SAN MARTÍN was a soldier of Spain for twenty years, and took part in all the wars his country fought in those turbulent times. Spain, no longer supremely confident of her destiny, changed her allegiances with bewildering rapidity—from Great Britain to France and back again. San Martín's history during those years must be reconstructed from the official record of his service, for outside of these documents, nothing definite is known of his personal life.

His first military adventure was a savage one, primitive warfare at its most violent, to which was added the horror of a natural cataclysm. In 1791, at the age of thirteen, his battalion was sent to Africa to reinforce the garrison at Oran. The Moors attacked, and the company of grenadiers defended the fort grimly. As they fought in the exhausting heat, an earthquake shook the town to pieces, but the Spaniards held out for thirty-six days, until their fort was a heap of ashes.

In San Martín's next experience he served with and against excellent generals. In 1793, Spain declared war on the French Revolutionary Directorate, and General Ricardos, a really great Spanish soldier-tactician, took his army across the Pyrenees to invade Roussillon in southern France. José took part in many battles; he was cited for bravery and was made a sub-lieutenant before he was sixteen. The Spanish offensive was crippled by the death of General Ricardos, but the army retired from France in perfect order. San Martín's firsthand experience in the scaling of high mountains to reach an enemy country was valuable training for his great Andean campaigns.

Great Britain, allied with Spain in this war, was dissatisfied with the peace terms, so the scenes soon shifted, and by the treaty of San Ildefonso in 1796, Spain became the ally of France against England. Early in 1797, the British attacked the Spanish squadron. José's regiment was stationed on the frigate *Santa Dorotea*, which was attacked by a powerful British ship carrying sixty-four cannon. After a desperate and gallant defense, to which the British paid tribute in their official report, the *Santa Dorotea* was captured.

In after life, San Martín paid for these years of strain, irregular hours and bad food with rheumatic and gastric pains that could be relieved only by opium.

In 1801 his regiment was sent to Portugal to fight the War of the Oranges and here he was made a second lieutenant in the Regiment of Murcia. It is a curious coincidence that the uniform of this regiment where the boy fought so gallantly was blue and white, the future colors of the flag of Argentina, carried by him in the wars of American independence.

Then came a few years of comparative quiet when, as captain, he was stationed at the garrison in Cadiz, where he remained until 1804. The garrison was more like a home than anything he had known in Spain. During 1802, a fierce epidemic of cholera visited Cadiz, and the

White City, "the island of chalk," became a place of groaning anguish and sudden wholesale death. There are brief glimpses of José in those years, flashes out of the dark here and there. On his military record it is noted that he received honorable mention for heroic services during the epidemic.

He does not seem to have had the usual officer's interest in pretty women. There is no record of any woman in his life in Spain, except a note found among the effects of a Spanish soldier during the war of independence in Peru. The note is signed "Pepa la Gaditana" (the woman of Cadiz). She tells her friend that if he should fall prisoner to the colonials, he should ask to be taken before José de San Martín and mention her name. She claims to have known him well in the old days at Cadiz, and she was evidently, as the Spanish say expressively, *de la vida alegre.*

"The whitest city in the world," was an oasis to José, scene of an all-too-brief breathing spell. It was the one period of his life in Spain to which he ever referred, and in later years it was his delight to tell his soldiers anecdotes of camp and garrison life there. He acquired the pithy, biting humor of the Andalusian peasant and he would pass judgment in terse, epigrammatic remarks. The Spanish historian Ciro Bayo, who has small liking for any of the Creole leaders, says that San Martín's manner of speech was that of an uncultivated gypsy. He was always an utter realist, and though it is untrue that he was uncultivated, he combined a soldier's impatience of sham with the shrewd, sarcastic wit of the children of the soil.

Furthermore, more important to his destiny, he had the

22

leisure in Cadiz to read those books which were spreading exciting new doctrines of liberalism and emphasizing the rights of man.

It was in Cadiz that José, at an age when friendships take strong root, formed associations that were to continue in the new world. Two of the friends he made here were Spaniards—General Ordonez and Don Alejandro Aguado, both to play important roles in his later life. Also in San Martín's circle was young García del Rio; and, most intimate and interesting friend of all, Bernardo O'Higgins, the illegitimate son of Ambrosio O'Higgins, that brilliant Irish adventurer who went out to South America as a peddler and died as Viceroy of Peru.

Bernardo, in Europe to finish his education, stood one day in a Cadiz crowd, enviously watching the Spanish troops marching to war. He noticed the striking, melancholy face of José de San Martín, and wondered who he was. Later the boys met and became devoted friends; this was one of the very few intimate friendships of San Martín's lonely life, for together they were to share the high adventure of the wars of liberation in South America.

In the circle of young Creoles in Spain, there was much talk of South America and especially of Francisco de Miranda, South America's Don Quijote, the Venezuelan patriot and soldier of fortune. Miranda resided in London from 1799 to 1805, and he was a tireless worker in the cause of independence. He called himself the agent of the South American colonies, and sought any and all opportunities to urge his schemes for revolution on the phlegmatic British statesmen. He would linger on street corners near the British Foreign Office, hoping to see

Mr. Pitt, the Prime Minister. The bored Pitt, unable to shake him, was forced to listen to Miranda's pleas and, chiefly to annoy Spain, gave him some encouragement.

It is supposed that Miranda came to Cadiz at that time to organize the political secret society known as the Lautaro Lodge; if he did, San Martín undoubtedly met him.

In 1806, Miranda conducted an unsuccessful filibustering expedition to Venezuela. A year later, the tireless veteran again turned up in London, as full of enthusiastic hope as Dickens' Micawber. This time he interested Sir Arthur Wellesley, afterward Duke of Wellington, in his scheme. Wellesley finally agreed to send an expedition of ten thousand soldiers to help Miranda's revolution. A fleet was assembled at Cork, thousands of Irish volunteers enlisted, and Wellesley was selected as commander. Miranda at last seemed to be in luck, but suddenly came events that changed the face of Europe. On July 4, 1808, because of the common peril from Napoleon, Great Britain and Spain made peace. All hope of British intervention in South America disappeared, and Miranda's mission was stillborn.

The Spanish royal family, now decadent and sinister, had fallen to pieces like a house of cards. Charles III slept among his ancestors in the grim Escorial, and Spain was governed by that picturesque, utterly worthless trio whom Goya's paintings reveal in all their frailties—Charles IV, the empty-minded simpleton, Maria Luisa, his termagant wife, and her lover, the handsome, stupid Manuel Godoy, who went by the title of Prince of the Peace and was married to the daughter of a Bourbon.

The best comment on that Queen of Spain was made

CHARLES IV OF SPAIN

by Napoleon when he saw her in Bayonne. "Maria Luisa has her past and her character written on her face; it surpasses anything you dare imagine." Her husband described to the astonished Napoleon the way he ran the Spanish empire. It was all so easy and pleasant. "I hunted all morning until dinner—then all afternoon until evening. Manuel told me things were going on all right, so I didn't bother." The quarrels of the old king, his strumpet wife and his villainous son Ferdinand, made Spain rock with laughter, but it was comedy that swiftly turned to tragedy. After the son forced the father to abdicate, Napoleon, watchful as a hawk, maneuvered them both into France, made them his prisoners, bullied Ferdinand into abdicating in his favor, and placed them in charge of Prince Talleyrand at his chateau. Under pretense of invading Portugal the French armies swarmed into Spain, occupied Madrid, and before Spain knew what it was all about, Joseph Bonaparte, Napoleon's brother, was proclaimed their king. It was blitzkrieg, as the nineteenth century knew it. Thus did four worthless human beings throw away the greatest empire the world had known since Rome.

In the hour when Spain realized how she had been betrayed by her rulers, the country was suddenly aroused by the brave alcalde of Mostoles, a small village outside Madrid. From alcalde to alcalde, his cry to arms was transmitted by swift-riding messengers. "The fatherland is in peril! Madrid perishes, a victim of French perfidy! Spaniards, come to her rescue!" A fury of resistance to the French swept over the land, not greatly affecting the court, but inflaming the masses of the people, the workers, the soldiers, the priests and the peasants. Spain was in peril!

A new spirit was abroad. José de San Martín, in Andalusia with his regiment at the time, was carried along on the wave of popular excitement. For years he had heard of the utter viciousness of the court, and great disillusionment had seized upon him, a disillusionment such as his simple father, living in happier days, had never known. He saw the idol's feet of clay, and realized how destitute the Spanish monarchy had come to be of anything that could be honored or respected. Before his keen, realistic vision vanished the mysterious majesty which had always enveloped the Spanish crown in the eyes of the Spanish colonials. He saw that the people had not only been abandoned, but had been delivered over to the enemy. It was only natural that San Martín and most of his young officer friends rallied to their defense.

At this time occurred an incident that affected San Martín's whole attitude towards questions of government for the rest of his life. Seville had declared against France. The Junta of Seville, attempting to carry on a Spanish government and resist Napoleon, sent the Count de Teva to Cadiz to move the insurrection of the city and add it to the Andalusian revolt. The officials of Cadiz, headed by General Solano, were in no hurry to join the revolt· and published a statement saying that time should be taken to map out an organized campaign. One reason for their hesitation was this: after several lean years, the city had a great harvest; if they declared war immediately, there would be no workers to gather it in. After all, the sovereigns had deserted Spain, and of their own free will.

26

Pondering these things, the officials demurred and hesitated.

General Solano, a fellow South American from Caracas, was acting Captain General of Andalusia, and San Martín was devotedly attached to him. Solano was ordered by the Junta, which had appointed him, to attack the French squadron anchored in the bay. He felt that the step was too drastic and asked for a few hours to consider. A paroxysm of fury at such hesitation swept the mobs of Cadiz. They broke into the arsenal, freed the prisoners and, failing to capture the French consul who had fled, marched to the house of General Solano in what is now Plaza Arguelles.

José was captain of the guard that day. At about four in the afternoon, the unsuspecting general was entertaining guests in the *sala*. Suddenly came hoarse cries from the street, the foreboding tramp of an advancing mob. José bolted the outer doors and stationed his guard on the defense. The rabble, clamoring for the blood of Solano, dragged up pieces of artillery to blast open the walls. Solano gave the order not to use force, but to hold the door while he attempted an escape over the roofs. This he did, and took refuge in the house of an Irish lady who was his neighbor. She concealed him, but a spy reported his hiding place to the mob. Roaring in on the unfortunate general, they dragged him down the street and stabbed him to death, screaming "Liberty! Liberty!"

San Martín never forgot the horror of that afternoon. The mob seemed to him a hydra. Were such people capable of governing themselves, infallible as the new enlightenment proclaimed them? Was democracy the

27

principle to regenerate a world in which monarchy had failed? "The best Government is not that which is most liberal in its principles, but one created by the philosophy of those who obey," he wrote to a friend in Chile long afterwards.

The memory of Solano always lingered. To the hour of his death, San Martín carried in his portfolio a black-banded miniature of his friend and general. Was *vox populi* truly *vox dei*? San Martín wondered.

Chapter V

THE LIBERTY OF MY NATIVE LAND

OTHERS beside Solano met the fate meted out to him who hesitated. Two other captains general were murdered by the mobs for not declaring against Napoleon. In Valencia in two days three hundred and thirty-eight persons, a whole colony of French merchants, fell victims to popular fury. A delegate was sent to England and was assured that Spain could draw on her for men and munitions. It was popular to describe the French as a race of antichrists and devils who should be relentlessly wiped off the face of the earth.

Napoleon's invasion of Spain was an important chapter in his duel to the death against Great Britain. In the building up of a continental bloc against her, his policy was to destroy the ancient Bourbon family in Naples and Spain, supplanting them with his own relatives, members of the new Napoleonic dynasty. The decadent Charles and Ferdinand had led him to suppose that the change would be a simple matter in Spain, and he failed utterly to realize the wild nationalism of their people, whom he considered supremely ignorant and contemptible.

The Junta of Seville was in complete charge of the patriots' conduct of the war, and entrusted the campaign in the south to General Francisco Javier Castaños, while Napoleon placed Dupont, one of his best generals, in

29

charge of the French in that section. Andalusia was important to him as it was the gateway to Africa, which could not be invaded without its possession. Then too the great importance of Cadiz as a naval base could not be overlooked, as it would form the western bulwark of his hegemony in the Continent.

After General Solano's murder, San Martín became cavalry captain in the regiment of Bourbon in the army of Andalusia, which joined the division commanded by the Marquis de Coupigny. In the first skirmish on the Guadalquivir River, he put to rout an advance French guard by leading his troops in a sabre charge at Arjonilla. In the *Gaceta Ministerial* of June 29, 1808, the young Captain praises the gallantry of his men. Juan de Dios, whom he cites for bravery in this despatch, saved his life at San Lorenzo, years later in the new world.

It is not the purpose of this biography to linger long over the Peninsular War, although it was the hard school that moulded the Conqueror of the Andes. The main body of the French army was in Central Spain, facing the high central plateau of the peninsula where every road continually crossed water over difficult passes. It was difficult to get reenforcements; swift, quick advances were impossible as, notwithstanding the improvements made by Charles III, the roads were nearly always in terrible condition. The whole mountain and river system lay at right angles across the main line of advance of the French army, so the invaders from the north had to ford every main river and climb the passes of every principal range. In the early nineteenth century, an army had to carry its food on wagon trains, drawn by long convoys of pack mules.

30

By the time enough food had been assembled to support a force, the enemy would get word of its position, which could only be held as long as the soldiers could be fed. Thus the French had to be constantly moving their forces through an arid desolate country, harassed mercilessly by hostile peasants. Furthermore, Portugal was still unsubdued, and General Wellington's British could constantly sally out of that country to attack the French flank. Having to protect themselves against these onslaughts, the French were never able to spare enough forces to complete the conquest of the south of Spain.

On the other hand, the French had the advantage of holding Madrid, the only important road centre, and thence they could operate in a vast semicircle against the Spaniards. Their troops were incomparably superior in training, experience and equipment. In 1808 the Spanish army only numbered 130,000 men. At the beginning of the campaign, high-priced contracts were made for the purchase of quantities of mules and wagons to carry munitions. The drivers, however, were not soldiers, and when they were in personal danger, they often ran away, abandoning the munitions to the enemy. The British generals openly expressed their contempt for their Spanish allies and were irritated by the ignorance of their officers. The training of officers, for which Charles III had made great plans, had been abandoned under the regime of the Prince of the Peace. In 1790 there had been five military colleges; Godoy had cut them to one small institution for the training of infantry and cavalry officers. The instruction of cadets was left to individual officers who gave them only the most elementary teaching. José

31

de San Martín, conscientious, fired with ambition, yet without formal training, had to learn how to be a competent leader through years of brutal, practical military service.

Yet to fight in the ragged Spanish army against the greatest man of the age was a sublime experience. The soldiers were undrilled and half clothed, the ranks depleted, the arsenals empty. The treasury was practically nonexistent, their rulers had abandoned them, everything had fallen into a state of chaos. In this pitiful army, however, lay the spark which fires those who fight for freedom. Their soil was being attacked and the Spaniard, who stands endless abuse from his own, rose to heights of unparalleled heroism struggling against the foreign invader. In sieges like Zaragoza, each street offered a new battle, each house meant a new siege. "Spain was the running sore that sapped my strength," said Napoleon in after years.

The name of the serious young Argentine leader begins to be heard on the public tongue. Step by step, he mounts the ladder during those gruelling years of constant physical danger. After the great Spanish victory at Bailen, which weakened the French power in Spain, José was given a gold medal for heroism under fire and was appointed lieutenant-colonel of cavalry. A year later he became the Marquis de Coupigny's aide-de-camp; and in July, 1811, he was made commander of the regiment of Saguntum Dragoons. The banner of this regiment displayed the sun, and had this caption, "It dissipates clouds and removes obstacles," a motto later used on the historic flag of the Army of the Andes.

Despite his youth, San Martín had now a long and dis-

32

SOLDIERS (POLISTAS) OF THE EAST BANK OF THE PLATA

tinguished record. A colonel, respected and honored, his future seemed boundless, particularly among officers not noted for conscientious work. He had fought with men of all nations, learned all types of warfare. Few soldiers possessed more thorough and varied training in actual war. He was very much more than a simple extravert. The idealism of old Castile, that scorned mere worldly power, lay strong within him, and his reflective moments taught him many things.

One thing he knew: Spain had no future whether Napoleon or Ferdinand ruled; the country would still be in the grip of tyranny. To save the young countries of America from this hopelessness, to make them independent lands free to work out their destinies—this almost superhuman task drew him irresistibly. It became a religious vocation, a fixed conviction. He had paid his debt to Spain, and her honors meant nothing.

San Martín did nothing impulsively. The decisions he made, like the battles he was to fight, were the product of long and careful consideration. He had never forgotten his country and had always looked on himself as an Argentinian. Now that her destinies were shaping, he longed to take part in them. The quiet years in the Cadiz garrison, when he pored over books of the new liberalism had, despite the shock of Solano's murder, produced their effect.

The young South Americans were on fire about the news from home, where the policies of the Central Spanish Junta were proving extremely unpopular. When word reached Argentina in 1810 that the French had overrun all Spain but a small strip around Cadiz, an open meeting

33

of the people in arms was held in Buenos Aires on May 25, and the first step was taken towards independence. The resignation of the Spanish Viceroy Cisneros and his cabildo was demanded and obtained, and a ten-man junta of the Province of the Plata was established, the members swearing with more or less sincerity to preserve the country for their "revered" King Ferdinand. This junta refused obedience to any junta set up in Spain, and assumed the full powers exercised up to this time by the Viceroy. May 25, 1810 marked the actual starting point for the South American Revolution whose fire was never once extinguished in Argentina, although uprisings in other states were temporarily stamped out.

Ships from the new world brought exciting news. The indefatigable Francisco de Miranda, after thirty-seven years in exile, had landed in Venezuela. On March 2, 1811, the first Venezuelan Congress assembled in Caracas. They pledged themselves to oppose France and to remain independent of any form of government in Spain, but stopped at an actual declaration of independence. However, the final step was taken on July 5, with the proclamation of the absolute independence of Venezuela from the Spanish empire.

Revolution burst upon Chile on September 18, 1810. On that day in the presence of a public town meeting, *cabildo abierto*, the Spanish Captain General Carrasco was forced to resign. A provisional junta of seven members was organized, which, not yet ripe for independence, still protested Chile's loyalty to imprisoned King Ferdinand. The country's population at that time numbered approximately a half million, including 100,000 Araucanian In-

34

dians, 300,000 *mestizos,* 150,000 Creoles, and 20,000 recently arrived Spaniards. There were three political groups. The small but powerful party of the Spaniards set themselves against all change; the moderate party of the landed Creole aristocracy felt timid about too much and too violent change, while the revolutionary party of a few talented young leaders swayed the popular masses to advocate a change that was an "all out" break from Spain.

The provinces of Chile elected delegates to a congress which met on July 4, 1811, to organize a more definite scheme of government. The moderate party controlled it, and they kept on expressing loyalty to King Ferdinand. A few weeks later, a brilliant, swaggering adventurer by the name of José Miguel Carrera landed in Chile. A native son, he had been serving in the Spanish army, but returned to his mother country with boundless plans for a glorious future. He appeared before the congress, described the frightful conditions in Spain, and, in an impassioned address, begged for American independence. He ended by offering his sword to the cause of liberty. The crowds went wild, and Carrera was the hero of the hour. He dissolved the congress and assumed dictatorial powers, but his selfish motives soon became so blatantly apparent that a faction of the more idealistic Chileans opposed him. Their leader was Bernardo O'Higgins, son of that amazing Irish peddler, "Father Paddy," who had died as Viceroy of Peru. Between the pro-Spanish faction and the split in the American faction, Chile rapidly drifted into civil war, and the sudden invasion of the country by the Viceroy of Peru made Carrera and O'Higgins realize that if they did not hang together, they would hang separately. Their forces hastily united. They went down to defeat in October, 1814, and the cause of Chilean independence was completely blotted out for several years.

War also blazed up in the La Plata region. Montevideo had from the first recognized the authority of the Spanish Junta. In January, 1811, the latter sent General Elió to South America as Viceroy of La Plata. He claimed Buenos Aires as his capital, but the people resisted his title violently and open warfare broke out between the two cities. The Portuguese court at Rio, seeing in the quarrel an opportunity for their own expansion, supported Elió, while Buenos Aires was aided by the guerrilla gaucho warriors of the country around Montevideo, who hated the royalist atmosphere in that city. In this fitful, confused civil war, Buenos Aires was also assisted for a while by a great but most eccentric gaucho chief, José Artigas, who declared against Spain. As an independent chief who commanded fanatical devotion from his hordes of Indian riders and gaucho cavalry, he kept up a constant guerrilla warfare all through the river country. He helped Argentina until 1814, when he turned against her and played a lone hand.

Of all the colorful leaders in the war of South American independence, this Uruguayan gaucho is the most picturesque. Completely honest, fiercely independent, he styled himself the Protector of Free Peoples, and received his followers seated on a bullock's skull, munching beef off a spit and drinking long draughts of gin from a cowhorn. He had drawn up a plan of independence, grant-

36

ing autonomous government to each state, "taking the United States as my model."

Spain's agents vainly tried to buy Artigas off. He was the perfect type of wild, liberty-loving gaucho, the man of the plains who would fight to the death against oppression. From his mud hut he sent out an unending stream of couriers with messages to Montevideo, to the provinces of the viceroyalty, to the Guarani missions, all stressing his defiance of the Spanish empire, arousing and exhorting timid patriots. Artigas also quarreled constantly with Buenos Aires—not that he advocated the independence of Uruguay, but rather that he desired complete provincial self-government in an Argentine nation.

Buenos Aires had summoned delegates from the cities of the old viceroyalty to its new junta, which had assumed the full powers of the Viceroy. After some objection, all the cities of the Argentine region accepted and elected delegates. Paraguay and Montevideo declined. In 1811 Buenos Aires signed a treaty acknowledging the separate existence of Paraguay. As most of Upper Peru was held by royal governors under the Viceroy of Peru, loyal to the Cadiz Regency, they also refused. The Argentinians promptly sent an army north, up the steep passes into Peru, and first blood in this war was spilled in a victory over the Spanish troops at Suipacha.

The triumph was short lived, as the Argentinians were soon driven back. Upper Peru (now Bolivia) could only be won and held by an army of mountaineers, and the men of Argentina were unused to the rarefied air of great heights. In this battleground the mountains rose like stupendous rocky fortresses, eight thousand to thirteen thousand feet above sea level. The Indian native peasantry was indifferent to a change of masters and more or less hostile. The country was utterly barren and the army, far from its base of supplies, suffered from exhaustion and mountain sickness. The struggle against the royalists for the possession of Upper Peru became a series of advances and retreats, the fitful guerrilla fighting. The royalists aimed to penetrate the high country to effect the capture of Buenos Aires with the aid of friendly Montevideo, while the Argentinians kept before their eyes the capture of Lima, to be achieved by piercing through this mountain country. Neither army ever attained its aim.

The picture presented by the new world in 1811 was too much for one of Argentine blood. San Martín was undergoing a terrible struggle. Unlike Francisco de Miranda, he was not a soldier of fortune, nor was he a gentleman of leisure like Simón Bolívar. To Miranda, Europe was only another adventurous checkerboard, and although he never forgot the goal of American independence, he was content to enjoy the passing moment. His loyalty was at the service of any power—the overloving Catherine of Russia or the revolutionary chiefs of France. Bolívar had no roots in the old world, but visited it as an interested onlooker, traveling with his tutor. To José de San Martín, however, Europe was home. Devotedly he had served Spain for twenty years and she had shown her gratitude. His heart was in Argentina because he felt, as years later Lincoln Steffens felt about Russia, that there lay a future that would work. A future under Spain meant at best a return of the "well-desired" Ferdinand and the old, stupid, feudal past. In after years he wrote, "Twenty years of honorable service had gained for me some consideration in spite of the fact that I was an American; I heard of the Revolution in South America and, forsaking my fortunes and my hopes, I desired only to sacrifice everything to promote the liberty of my native land."

The decision was made, and he prepared for departure. Great caution was necessary, although there was as yet no suspicion of his change of heart. He petitioned the regency to be allowed to retire from the army and go to Lima, "in order to look after the interests of my two brothers now serving in the Spanish army." The report on the application was favorable; it stated that the officer making the request had served twenty-two years with the army and had achieved outstanding distinction. This report was sent to the council of the regency, to the secretary of state and the department of war.

It can never be known, from existing information, whether San Martín really intended to sail for Lima and then changed his mind. Certainly the poor San Martín boys never owned a foot of ground in Peru. He could have sailed for Peru without arousing suspicion, as it was a viceroyalty utterly loyal to Spain, and his own devotion to the royalist cause was then unquestioned. Instead, he prepared for secret departure. A falsified passport for England was obtained from Sir Charles Stuart, British diplomatic agent, and San Martín was aided in his plans by Lord Macduff, a noted Englishman, who had come to the Peninsula to fight against Napoleon, and whom San Martín had met in the Lautaro Lodge at Cadiz. The sudden change of plans probably meant that some rumor about him had reached the Spanish authorities. He was forced to act quickly; disguising himself as a peasant, he left secretly for London, never again to see the country to which he had given his youth.

Chapter VI

LAUTARO LODGE

EVERY STUDENT of South American independence remembers the rather mysterious politico-Masonic lodge known as *Logia de Lautaro,* founded in 1812 in Buenos Aires, which had for its object the establishment of a republican form of government in Argentina. Its immediate origin is to be found in Cadiz in 1808–1809. It is said that Francisco Miranda, traveling incognito, went there to talk over the independence of Spanish America with a group of American-born officers who were then stationed at Cadiz. On this visit he is supposed to have founded a branch of a secret lodge established by him in London in 1801, of which Carlos Alvear, the Chilean patriot Carrera, and even the great Bolívar are said to have been members. Miranda had been interested in Masonry for many years, and in 1796 had affiliated himself with the French Rite into which he had been introduced by his intimate friend General Lafayette. When this first Lautaro Lodge was chartered in London, it was formed as a Masonic body independent of the regularly established Masonry in either France or England, where the order was at that time in a condition of confusion. Furthermore, as the Lautaro Lodge was intended to serve the end of political independence, Miranda felt that a series of thirty-three degrees

41

would only serve to delay the availability of the men he chose to work towards this purpose. The lodges in London and Cadiz followed the general plan of French Masonry, in which five degrees were included.

This *Sociedad Lautaro* at Cadiz acted as a clearing-house for all prominent Americans in that city, and when there remained no doubt of their loyalty and active devotion to the patriot cause, they were invited to affiliate. In the first degree the neophyte was asked to pledge his life and fortune to work for American independence. In the next degree he made a profession of democratic faith, swearing to recognize as lawful government in the new world only one chosen by the free will of the people, and he gave his promise to strive for the establishment of a republican system in both Spain and America. In the third degree the candidate was given tasks that involved the propagation of these ideals. In the fourth grade it was the initiate's duty to influence the colonial administration in favor of the cause and, exercising extreme caution, he was to attempt to win over public officials who could aid in a successful revolt. In the fifth or last degree, military plans for revolution were discussed, also the institutions which were to be established in case of success, and suitable candidates to take charge of them. These fifth-degree men were allowed to work in any grade, and the affiliates of one degree had no knowledge of the names of members of other classes. In fact, so vital was the necessity of secrecy in the heart of absolutist Spain that as little as possible was trusted to writing, and all names of workers and their tasks were committed to memory. Rarely did more than seven brothers hold a meeting. Such assemblies were held in the utmost privacy, and the place of meeting was constantly changed.

The Cadiz Lodge was an independent Masonic body. Although there were many powerful men in British Masonry who were friendly, it would have been impossible for them to affiliate formally, as the British Government had allied itself with Spain against Napoleon. One of the tasks with which the Cadiz Lodge concerned itself was the smuggling into America of books by French Liberals, as they felt that a perusal of Voltaire, Montesquieu, Rousseau and the Encyclopedists would rouse the educated Creoles at home from their apathy. As permission was freely granted to send over sacred vessels and church ornaments without inspection, many a French book, slipped into the ecclesiastical shipments, found its way into eager South American hands, thus escaping the fate of being burnt or fed to llamas.

San Martín had joined the Cadiz Lodge during his garrison days. When he arrived in London, he carried letters from a fellow member, Lord Macduff, an Englishman who had given distinguished service against Napoleon in the Peninsula. Through him he was introduced to the London Lautaro Lodge into which he was initiated, together with Martin Zapiola, Baron Holmberg and other military and naval officers. Creole reunions were constantly held in the famous house in Grafton Street, where the old master, Miranda, had lived in restless exile, and sooner or later every distinguished South American in Europe came to its door. Here was the European clearinghouse for news of the revolution; the Creole visitors talked and lived in its atmosphere, and they visioned not a narrow

43

national upheaval, but the revolution of the American continent.

In January, 1812, a small group of Creoles left London on the *George Canning,* bound for Buenos Aires, where they arrived on March 12, after fifty days at sea. Among them were José de San Martín and Carlos de Alvear. The latter, who was to play an adventurous part in the revolution, was a handsome, vivacious aristocrat, whose wealthy family possessed great influence in Buenos Aires and whose path was to cross rather unfortunately with that of San Martín.

A trip on a sailing vessel from Europe to South America in 1812 was a strain on the toughest constitution. Fresh food lasted about ten days, after which the menu consisted of a soup of dried beans, smoked pork, dried fish and sea biscuits. Sanitary conditions are best left to the imagination. The handful of passengers helped the sailors with the chores or gossiped through long hours over wine and cigars. On the *George Canning,* Alvear's pretty young wife was the life of the company, and the Creole gentlemen entertained her with tales and songs. There was a young German Baron on board, Von Holmberg, on his way to join the war of independence; his fund of curious folklore from his country intrigued the passengers.

They were all full of enthusiasm for the coming struggle, and there was much talk about Argentina. The consensus of opinion was that they must create a firm central government, combat the tendency to loose federalism which only meant disorder and disobedient leaders in the provinces, completely reorganize the army, and establish

44

the Lautaro Lodge in order to unify the whole scheme of independence. Each man had his own ideas, and they repeatedly interrupted one another; the man in the group who said least was José de San Martín.

He was then thirty-four years of age, tall and powerful, with the unmistakable air of the military. Twenty years of life in the open air had bronzed his complexion to so deep an olive that he was sometimes called *El Indio*. His nose was aquiline, his mouth small and well formed, his dark eyes unusual for their size and piercing intensity. His manners were unobtrusive and simple, but he kept people at a distance and he kept his thoughts to himself. Dr. Mitre, the Argentine historian, calls him a wise and keen observer of human nature. Few could ever penetrate the reserve that concealed an iron singleness of purpose. His will had made a silent dedication of his life to the cause of the independence of the continent. To him nothing else mattered. No crusader ever embarked on the quest for the Holy Sepulchre with a more unswerving purpose. Not worldly distraction, political ambition, mental nor physical suffering, not even human affection could ever sway him from the path. His vision was not only of an independent Argentina, but an independent America, building up its civilization freed from the ambitions of a greedy Europe.

Landing in Buenos Aires was a complicated business in those days. The outer roads of the harbor were nine miles from the town. Here vessels were compelled to anchor, and passengers were rowed to the beach. Even small boats could not approach nearer than fifty yards to the shore, so passengers had to change once more and stand in high-wheeled wooden carts, drawn by two horses, on one of which an Indian was mounted. Then, at breakneck speed, the carts were driven through the water to the rough stone landing.

The Buenos Aires of 1812, which was to play so large a part in the history of independence, was an unpretentious, democratic city with neither the romantic charm nor the feudal caste systems of Lima and Rio de Janeiro. At that time it had about sixty-five thousand inhabitants. The streets were straight and broad for a Spanish city, unpaved in the middle, and with footpaths on either side. Most of the houses were one-story structures, the poorer ones of mud, others of brick and lime. There was ordinarily no glass, and the windows were heavily grated. Many of the public and religious structures were made of a beautiful white stone found in a plain not far from town, and when the bleak wind called the *pampero* blew down upon the city, it bleached even more deeply their shining whiteness. Almost every house had its garden and its latticed balconies; and in Buenos Aires grew the largest carnations in the whole world. There were few negro slaves, and they were treated with kindness, often being employed as overseers of farms or herds of cattle. Compared with other parts of the country, there was little class feeling throughout Argentina. It had not yet emerged from its colonial, Arcadian simplicity.

A brief note in the official *Gazette* announced the arrival of the group which had come to offer their services to the cause of freedom. The news created quite a stir and considerable suspicion. Sharp-tongued citizens remarked that they were probably spies and would bear keen watching. The only one known in town was Carlos de Alvear. Since

46

San Martín had been until so recently a colonel in the Spanish army, suspicion centered on him. It was rumored he was still in the pay of the Spanish government. The newcomers presented themselves at the fort, the old residence of the Viceroys, where San Martín laid before the authorities his record of military services; the record characterized him as "single, of a noble family, son of a Captain." The triumvirate Pueyrredon, Rivadavia and Chiclana, then governing Buenos Aires, after careful deliberation, confirmed him in the rank of lieutenant-colonel of cavalry "because of his merits, achievements and military knowledge," and later made him chief of the squadron of cavalry, which it became his task to reorganize.

His regiment of cavalry was known as the Mounted Grenadiers, and they wrote their name in the history of the continent. With this picked body of men, he made the Argentine cavalry famous, and they served with distinction in every battle of the revolution from 1812 to 1827. It was a thrill to the youth of Buenos Aires to be drilled by this famous soldier of Spain, who had fought the best men of Napoleon. He was a kindly taskmaster, but relentless, for his clear mind recognized how much there was to do, the intense training and organization needed. If they delayed too long, the Napoleonic wars would end, leaving Spain free to ship the bulk of her trained troops for service in the new world. Although the war of independence had begun, there was no definite plan of operation, no efficient director of campaign. The Grenadiers were given practical instruction in military tactics, and in the technique of war. San Martín himself chose the soldiers and officers, and constantly tested the nerves of the young students by fre-

47

quent ambushes and night surprises. The long sabre used by Napoleon's cuirassiers was introduced so "they could cut off the heads of their Gothic enemies as one would sever a watermelon." Godos, or Goths, San Martín's nickname for the royalists, was commonly used in the patriot army, much as the word Boche was used in World War I.

Like Frederick the Great, he picked his men tall. His mounted Grenadiers soon became the pride of the city. They were quartered in the Retiro, the old slave market, then known as Campo de Marte. The river ran near by, and along its banks was the Alameda, the only fine avenue for taking the "good airs" of the city. Señoritas of aristocratic families, chaperoned by their dueñas, would drive by in the afternoon hoping to catch a glimpse of the grave, handsome commander and the towering Grenadiers.

They were the talk of the town, and it was a holiday when they gave exhibitions of their riding and fencing. The officers had a strict code of behavior which they themselves applied in a system of self-government, holding council meeting every Sunday at which San Martín presided. Any one guilty of unbecoming conduct was expelled from the regiment, and one of the most unpardonable offenses was to refuse a challenge to duel if given by an equal.

The Chilean historian Vicuña MacKenna has said that San Martín brought to the service of the revolution two powerful elements: military strategy, unknown before, imported at that time from Europe, and the secret Lautaro Lodge, which he founded, with the aid of Alvear and Zapiola, soon after reaching Buenos Aires in 1812. The object of this new Lodge in the city was to shape and direct

48

LANDING PLACE, BUENOS AIRES, 1820

the future course of the revolution. A Masonic lodge had been founded in 1801, but had dispersed on the death of its leader.

The liberal group in Buenos Aires were calling for a constitutional convention; and while the masses restlessly demanded more power, they were drifting and helpless without the direction of a small, experienced group. The fall of the Viceroys had destroyed the spirit of authority, and the excited people crowded into the *cabildo abierto* where there were endless debates on government questions; but while they wrangled, the war languished without hope of success.

The new Lautaro Lodge set up its quarters in an old house situated in what is now Balcarce Street. Under the guidance of the "triangle," San Martín, Alvear and Zapiola, its membership rapidly increased. Because of the founders' qualities of leadership, the finest type of youth was attracted to the lodge, and enthusiasm for the war revived and soon reached fever pitch. As in Cadiz, the initiate swore to devote his life and fortune to American independence, conducting himself both as a citizen and Mason with justice and honor. The members were known to one another as "the brothers." The motto of the Lodge was, Union, Strength, Virtue; in communications between the members it was referred to by the sign O-o. There were two chambers in the Lodge. The Lautaro, known as the blue, bestowed the first three degrees of Masonry; in the superior or rose chamber, advanced members were awarded the fourth and fifth degrees. This higher chamber was called by San Martín the "Grand Lodge of Buenos Aires," and it was this section that directed the revolution, not the

Lautaro part, which had no share in the deliberations of the advanced body, although they were closely united. Only when members, because of marked ability, were advanced to the rose, were they informed of the political policies of the Grand Lodge.

Although much criticism of Lautaro Lodge has been expressed, and many tales of its political intrigues exist, it did accomplish the shaping and organizing of the revolution, which, when San Martín returned to Argentina, was in a critical state. It was due to the determination of its members that the Argentine-Chilean alliance, the salvation of American independence, was initiated and maintained. The Buenos Aires Lodge remained in communication with Spanish liberals on the Peninsula, and kept three Argentine secret agents on the ground at Cadiz, where lodge activities were instrumental in preventing the Spanish government from sending its projected expeditionary force to reconquer the Plata district.

An important aid towards the more effective organization of the war was the establishment by the Buenos Aires Lodge of the secret lodges in Mendoza, and in Santiago, where Bernardo O'Higgins was the founder. Through the collaboration of the brothers in Buenos Aires with those in Mendoza, San Martín was able to finance the Army of the Andes and send the Army of Liberation into Peru. Here the patriots Riva Agüero, Francisco de Paula Quirós and Fernández Lopez Aldana had formed a Masonic lodge to render the people receptive to the idea of independence. This lodge came to include affiliates even in the state offices, and these kept the patriots constantly informed of the Viceroy's plans. Furthermore, when San Martín entered Lima, it was the Buenos Aires lodge that insisted that he assume the Protectorship of Peru to preserve the country from anarchy. This laid him open to endless vilification among his enemies as a betrayer of democracy, and the decision seems unwise in the light of later events.

San Martín attempted always to live up to the ideals of the Lautaro Lodge, as did also that other very prominent member, Juan Pueyrredon, Supreme Director of Argentina. On the other hand, Carlos Alvear was shameless in his use of the society as a stepping stone for his own advancement. Twenty-five years after San Martín's entrance into Lima, when he was an exile in Paris, the British General Miller wrote him for data on the Lodge and its part in the war of independence. He replied: "I do not consider it fitting to discuss the least detail concerning the Lodge of Buenos Aires; these are strictly private matters and although they have exercised and still do exercise great influence in the events of the revolution in that part of America, they could not be revealed without a breach on my part of the most sacred pledges." Thus spoke the devoted son of Argentine Masonry.

Chapter VII

SAN MARTÍN'S GRENADIERS

S AN MARTÍN had no experience in formal society, but he had a natural dignity that made him at home in any circle. Women were intrigued by his reserve and his reputation as a gallant fighter. His very avoidance of women shed a mysterious glamour on him, and they were distinctly interested, but rather awed, by him. Largely through Carlos de Alvear, he was introduced to the social world of Buenos Aires and was soon invited to evening parties and fiestas. He danced well and was extremely courteous. Among the houses where he was made welcome was that of Don Antonio José de Escalada—a beautiful home in the neighborhood of the cathedral. This gentleman had been a merchant, was very friendly to the patriot cause and had been for many years an intimate friend of all their leaders. In 1812, Rivadavia and the other triumvirs, the young Alvears and the army officers, used to frequent the evening salons held at the house. The formal manners of the viceroyalty were still in vogue, although the ideas expressed were the liberal ones of the revolution. Dr. Rojas, in his biography of San Martín, *Saint of the Sword*, says that there was an atmosphere both patriarchal and courtlike about the lovely drawing rooms of the Escalada family. There were glittering crystal chandeliers in the great rooms, which were carpeted with heavy blue silk

52

and fragrant with flowers. There was much gayety there in the evenings, when the young ladies would play the harpsichord, sing to the Andalusian guitar and dance minuets with the patriotic officers.

Don Antonio de Escalada had two daughters by his second wife, Doña Tomasa de la Quintana, who bore the poetical names of Maria de las Nieves and Maria de los Remedios. Remedios became the betrothed of San Martín very shortly after making his acquaintance. The little *novia* was not much more than fifteen, and had been completely sheltered and petted by her adoring parents. She loved dancing, which she did exquisitely, pretty clothes, and jasmine flowers, which she twined in her dark hair. Her portrait in the Museo Histórico of Buenos Aires shows a big-eyed, sweet-looking young Spanish girl with an expression of appealing innocence. San Martín's enemies said that on his part it was a marriage of worldly and political considerations, but if one reflects on Remedios' personality, this does not appear true. Her innocence charmed the austere colonel, whose life had been a kaleidoscope of camps and battles. She was different from anyone he had ever known. What matter if she were not in any way his intellectual equal, or if her character were too immature to fit her to be a great leader's wife? He had the old-fashioned Latin attitude towards women. As he later wrote in the instructions for his daughter's education, she was to learn enough to enable her to be "a tender mother and a good wife." Remedios' limitations were great, and her marriage to a man whose life kept him away for years at a time could not have been a happy one. Despite rumors to the contrary, she was always devoted and adoring. In her husband's relentless pursuit of his high task, no woman could have been vitally important; but he ordered inscribed on her simple tomb in the Recoleta Cemetery of Buenos Aires, these words, which show that she always occupied a deep, small corner of his heart: "Here lies Remedios Escalada, wife and friend of General San Martín."

Their wedding was celebrated on September 12, 1812, in the Cathedral of Buenos Aires, the sponsors for the young couple being that rising young politician and Grenadier, Carlos de Alvear, and his wife Doña Carmen. There was a merry fiesta at the Escalada mansion and the élite of the city crowded about offering their good wishes.

There was only a brief period of quiet before the pressure of ominous events distracted the bridegroom's attention from his child-wife. There were two factions in Buenos Aires; one, liberal-democratic, stood for a centralized popular government called "unitarism," with Buenos Aires exercising control over the provinces, and acting as a successor to the Spanish viceroyalty. The conservative group, on the other hand, catered to the provinces, where political leaders, intent on their own future, were making their appearance and telling the people that they were being deprived of their liberties by the politicians in Buenos Aires. The government was in the hands of a triumvirate who had not fulfilled their promise to call the national congress which the people of Argentina had been incessantly demanding, a congress which should include the provinces as well as the city of Buenos Aires. In the meanwhile, the three triumvirs, Sarratea, Chiclana and

Pueyrredon, continued governing as arbitrary dictators, and the general feeling throughout the old viceroyalty was that the people had been cheated of the reforms promised by the revolution.

There was deep dissatisfaction among the liberal elements of the city, many of whom, including San Martín and his friends, belonged to a newly formed literary society which anxiously followed the course of events. One day when the city council was meeting, the Regiment of Mounted Grenadiers marched into the Plaza de la Victoria and stood at attention. They sent a messenger into the council, who stated that it was the will of the people that the resignation of the triumvirate should be demanded, and that a new group should be appointed, pledged to the immediate calling of a national congress. The Council hesitated, but San Martín and Alvear appeared, urging them to haste as the populace was growing impatient and could not be controlled. Meekly they complied, deposed the triumvirate for a new trio—Passo, Rodriguez Peña and Alvarez Jonte. All citizens in the provinces and city of Buenos Aires could exercise the right of suffrage indirectly. Buenos Aires was to elect four delegates, while each of the provincial capitals and Tucumán were to elect two delegates to a national congress. It was a great liberal victory.

The congress, under the title of the General Assembly of the United Provinces, met on January 31, 1813. No constitution was enacted by this body, but they passed many laws, immediately enforced, implying independence from Spain, although it was still not declared in so many words. The coat of arms of Spain was no longer used; the king's effigy was effaced from the coins and replaced by the seal

55

of the United Provinces, consisting of a sun and a liberty cap. Titles of nobility were abolished. All children born from that time were considered free, a national anthem was proclaimed, and the members of congress named themselves the Deputies of the Nation. The blue and white flag, which General Belgrano had devised in 1812, became the banner of the Argentine, and for the first time no mention was made of the "much desired" King Ferdinand. Although informally as yet, Argentina had become a free nation.

Later, the system of triumvirate government was felt to be impractical and unstable, so a one-man executive took its place, with the title of Director of the United Provinces of the River Plata; he was to govern with the aid of a council of state. Carlos Alvear's uncle, Gervasio Posadas, became the first director of what was left of the old viceroyalty of La Plata.

San Martín's firm hand can be seen in the deposition of the first triumvirate and in the radical change in policy of the second one. He realized that a definite stand must be taken for freedom from Spain, for this indecision was creating widespread defection from the patriots' ranks. "Until the present," he said with his hard common sense, "the United Provinces have fought for a cause which nobody knows, without flag and without a statement of principles which would explain the origin and tendencies of the insurrection. It is necessary that we call ourselves independent that we may be known and respected."

Meanwhile the Spanish royalists stationed across the river at Montevideo carried on a reign of terror in the districts along the Plata and Paraná. Swiftly marching

BALLING OSTRICHES

troops burned villages, stole property and murdered the helpless country people.

Spies reported at Buenos Aires that an even fiercer foraging expedition was on the way. A flotilla of about fifteen vessels was creeping up the river, hoping to land their men, strip the Argentine side of all provisions, at the same time closing the trade route to Paraguay. San Martín, given complete charge of the defense, ordered his Grenadiers to follow him out of the city. They were about to have their first taste of war, and he was happy to be given a call to action. Jealous rumors had increased about his being a spy for Spain. They had been reported to him, and he was in a mood of black depression.

The season was oppressively hot, but the Grenadiers, under cover of darkness, rode rapidly until they were opposite the flotilla and could observe it without being themselves seen in the thick underbrush. The Spaniards seemed to be making for San Lorenzo. On the heights, a lonely watchtower, stood the ancient Franciscan cloister of San Carlos, and San Martín decided to use it as a reconnoitering spot, suspecting—with good reason—that the enemy would stop to loot it.

The famous British traveler, William Robertson, happened to be passing down the river road on his way to Paraguay; as he dozed in his carriage, he was aroused by the tramping horses of the Grenadiers. Taking them for robbers, he was highly alarmed until he recognized San Martín, with whom he had a slight acquaintance. Hearing of the adventure they were bound on, Robertson asked permission to join them, and it was about midnight when they rode up to the cloister. The flotilla was nearing the bank. The Grenadiers were stationed on guard at the doors, ready to rush on the enemy, whose dim lanterns outlined the boats then anchoring. It was for all the world like the Greeks on the alert to pour out of the wooden horse of Troy, wrote Robertson. San Martín sat rigid in the belfry, straining his eyes to count the Spanish troops who were beginning to climb the heights. The right moment came at last. Drawing his curved sabre, he descended the stairs, remarking to Robertson, "In two minutes more we shall be upon them." He passed the word to the Grenadiers. The trumpets sounded the advance as his men galloped furiously down the hill. There followed a wild hand-to-hand conflict, but the Goths, though caught completely by surprise, held firm and turned their cannon on the Grenadiers. San Martín's horse fell, dragging his rider down and pinning him to the ground. Excited shouts showed that the enemy knew the chief was at their mercy. A Spanish soldier rushed forward savagely to finish him with a bayonet thrust. Then it was that young Sergeant Juan Bautista Cabral threw himself in front of the bayonet and saved his chief, but left unguarded his own defense. He fell, mortally wounded, just as the royalists broke and fled down to the river. The fierce enthusiasm of the Grenadiers had brought them an easy victory.

Juan Cabral died two hours later, happy in the knowledge that they had triumphed and that he had saved his chief, who knelt at his side, whispering his gratitude.

In the shade of a spreading pine tree, still preserved as a patriotic landmark, San Martín dictated the news of the battle. Although it was only a skirmish, it marked a definite turn for the better in the epic of Argentine independence. It marked also the beginning of San Martín's ascendancy as a leader in the affairs of Argentina; and, inevitably, his exposure to attack by those who had selfish interests to satisfy. The lack of stability in the country, the violent individualism of Creoles of Spanish blood freed from the controlling dictatorship of the old Spanish monarchy, the presence of large groups of ignorant mestizos and other half-breeds who could be played off against each other—these factors provided a fertile breeding ground for politicians, in the worst sense of that word. They were the forerunners of the *caudillos,* or political bosses who have created revolution after revolution and have been the curse of South America since its independence.

Buenos Aires had several clever Creoles in its public life who were on the alert to benefit themselves during this period of turmoil, but they were startled from their intrigues when it became apparent that San Martín was coming to the fore as a leader. The mysterious man from Spain would bear watching. They had an uneasy feeling that he would not be easy to manage, and this deadened any elation they might have felt at his successful routing of the royalists.

Chapter VIII

ADVENTURES IN PERU

ALTHOUGH THE skirmish in which San Martín routed the royalists was his first action in the new world, an Argentinian army in the north had been doggedly trying for months to invade Peru through the Andes. Their goal was Lima, the capital and citadel of the Spanish empire. Lima was loyal to the crown, and seemingly impregnable within her protecting circle of giant mountains.

General Belgrano led the army in the north and at first met with success. After a savage struggle, he captured the highland fortress of Salta where the royalist general who, like Belgrano, was a Creole, closed the pact of surrender by an embrace in the presence of both armies. The three thousand Gothic soldiers were given their freedom on swearing never again to take up arms against Argentina. But Belgrano, unsophisticated and honest, was too lenient for the type of struggle with which he was faced. These soldiers broke their word immediately on being released and returned to the main royalist forces, asking for more weapons to fight the rebel Creoles.

The tables turned against the patriots. The natives were almost always hostile, the royalists were firmly entrenched everywhere. A change of masters meant nothing to the apathetic Indians of Peru. They were friendly enough to

Spain and indifferent about the struggle. As the patriot army carried insufficient supplies, they had to live off the country and came to be cordially disliked as a band of outlaws. General Belgrano was badly defeated, the enemy recaptured Salta, and in January, 1814, San Martín was sent up to the mountains with reinforcements.

Ostensibly he was sent to help the rebel cause; actually he was sent to get him out of Buenos Aires, for certain men resented his growing popularity. The leading spirit in this scheme to oust him was the aristocratic Carlos de Alvear, San Martín's former comrade, who raged inwardly to see the respect paid to the quiet, shabby man he had always treated with patronizing condescension. Intensely ambitious and a member of the most influential family in Buenos Aires, Alvear thought to have his friend permanently shelved in a military deadlock, so he secured his transfer to aid Belgrano. On the surface he affected the old friendship, wishing San Martín a speedy success with effusive cordiality. But as soon as San Martín was out the door, Alvear remarked to his friends, "That man has shot his bolt."

San Martín and Belgrano had had much correspondence with one another and were very eager to meet. Belgrano had been a school teacher before the war. His calibre may be judged from the fact that after the victory of Salta, he refused the forty thousand pesos voted him by the Assembly of Buenos Aires and asked that the money be used to establish four elementary public schools.

Ever since he had read of San Martín's arrival in Argentina he had pinned his faith on him as the powerful leader they so badly needed. He went out to meet San Martín

61

and embraced him like an old friend. When the latter said he had come to place himself in Belgrano's service, the general protested, "You are to be not only my friend, but my teacher, my companion, and my chief if you wish." He felt that the newcomer's tactical knowledge and European military experience were so vital to success that he insisted that San Martín take over the command, which he finally assumed in January, 1814.

The war in the mountains of Peru dragged on to a hopeless stalemate. The object of the Goths was to break through to Buenos Aires, holding Montevideo as a base of supplies; the patriots hoped ultimately to end the war by the capture of Lima. Neither side was ever successful in this mountain campaign, but in 1814, the condition of the patriot army was especially desperate. The army had not been paid, they were inadequately equipped and their clothes were reduced to rags. Not only were the men untrained, the officers were incompetent and utterly discouraged. It seemed impossible to penetrate Upper Peru, that precipitous mountain land which separated the territories of Spain from Argentina. The Spaniards had with them a body of loyal native Indians, savage fighters, hardened to all privations, and, most important of all, at home in the dizzy altitudes where plainsmen gasped for breath and suffered excruciating headaches. Such was the chaos facing San Martín, the new commander of the army in Peru.

In his steady, methodical manner, he set up an entrenched camp at Tucumán and began military training, featuring the French cavalry tactics which had been the glory of Napoleon's army. He pointed to his Grenadiers as an example of what could be accomplished with South

American youth. Belgrano was one of the first to register for his class. To San Martín came also for training the famous Martin Güemes, with his band of gauchos. These men, mostly mestizos, were later to hold the frontier and become the terror of the Goths. Riding their horses at full speed down the rough mountain passes, they created panic when they dashed down on the enemy. Their most feared weapon was the *boleadora*—a stone ball on the end of a rope. Used as a lasso, it could bring the swiftest cavalry to earth.

Two anecdotes illustrate the spirit of the gaucho of the revolution. An advance detachment of Spaniards arrived at one of their small towns. One gaucho said to another, "We must attack this trash and drive it out."

"Yes, but with what weapons?" asked the other.

"With those that we take from them, of course."

And a Spanish general arriving with his troops at a miserable ranch house heard a woman shouting, "Boy, run and tell your father the Goths are here." A tiny child, not more than four years old, leaped on an unsaddled horse and galloped away. The gaping general cried, "Such a people is unconquerable." *

In April, 1814, four months after he took command, San Martín fell ill; he vomited blood profusely. The doctors thought he was tubercular and said that he had not long to live. As he did live to a ripe age, his trouble was

---

* General John Miller, who aided San Martín, wrote: "The gauchos kept men constantly on the highest trees to watch every movement of the royalists or to receive communications from friends in the town. Royalists who straggled to a small distance were invariably cut off. On some of the trees bells were hung; and tolling them the gauchos would call out to the Spaniards, 'Come, Goths, and hear Mass.' " *Memoirs*, Vol. I, p. 88.

probably gastric ulcers. He had lived a life of unusual hardship. In all his twenty years in the Spanish army, although he suffered from chronic rheumatism and asthma, he had not asked for one leave. In his new life in Argentina, he had been under continual nervous tension, the result of having to adapt himself to a new environment, defend himself against intrigue, and accomplish the results he so intensely desired. In Tucumán his illness became so serious that it was rumored among his soldiers that his days were numbered; he was probably the victim of a nervous collapse, aggravated by gastric disorders.

The physician who attended San Martín was an American, Don Guillermo Collisberry, a native of Philadelphia, who had made a reputation in South America as an excellent medical man. With his red hair and blue eyes, he was a striking figure as he wandered about the streets of Tucumán. Tormented with insomnia, San Martín turned over his command temporarily to Colonel Don Francisco de la Cruz, and retired to La Ramada, a farm near Tucumán, where he could lie on a wide balcony and look at the Andes. As he lay there, he had the satisfaction of knowing that the new guerrilla warfare he had instituted under the leadership of Martin Güemes was at least keeping the royalists checked. From his sick bed he kept in touch with affairs in Upper Peru, in Argentina and Chile, while night and day his uncanny mathematical mind was studying over the plan of the revolution as if it were a checkerboard.

He had devious ways of arousing the mestizos. One day a Creole peon on the ranch where he was staying complained to him that he had been cruelly beaten by the overseer who was a Goth.

FERDINAND VII OF SPAIN, PORTRAIT, BY J. GIL DE CASTRO,
NOW IN SANTIAGO

"The Goth did well to beat you," replied the General, without smiling.

"But why, sir?" asked the peon, not understanding such a sentiment from the great defender of the rights of Creoles.

"Because if one man hits another, it is because the other stands for it. And if that Goth struck you, and you allowed him to, you must take the consequences."

The next day the peon sought out the overseer and beat him severely.

In 1814 there flashed on San Martín's mind the only scheme of securing the liberty of his America. In April, in one of his rare bursts of confidence, he wrote to a friend that the campaign in Upper Peru would get nowhere. It would never amount to more than defensive warfare. Lima and Lima alone was the keystone of the war. The mountain fighting must be abandoned, leaving the brave gauchos under Martin Güemes and two battalions of seasoned veterans to hold the frontier. "To think of anything else is to insist on throwing money and men down a well.

"I have already told you my plan in strict confidence," continues this very important letter to Nicolas Peña. "My convictions remain unchanged. A small and well-disciplined army in Mendoza, the passage over the Andes to Chile, and there finish with the Goths. This would stamp out the anarchy which reigns there. Then the Chileans, in establishing a stable government, would become a reliable friend. Allying our forces, we would sail over the sea and take Lima. Until then, the war will not be finished."

Mendoza lay near the Chilean border, about seven hundred miles west of Buenos Aires. It was separated from the sea by the towering Andes and the narrow strip of Chile. With Martin Güemes and his gauchos protecting the northern frontier of Argentina against invasion, the enemy could be surprised in Chile and the war won almost at a single blow, but San Martín knew that if he urged such a plan in 1814, he would have been taken for a complete madman. Three years were to go by before he made his contemporaries realize that in this plan lay the only possible solution.

In San Martín, still waters ran deep, and during the three years, he made his own preparations. The strictest caution had to be observed; a word of his definite program to the Spaniards and all would be lost. While it was impossible to conceal the army's preparations from the enemy, the time and place of striking remained a complete mystery. And there was need for haste, the utmost haste. San Martín knew that the moment the Napoleonic war was over, the whole Spanish army would be released for service against the rebels in the new world.

In April, 1814, he laid down his command as head of the army in Peru. In August of that year, the Buenos Aires government, at that time under a one-man executive, acceded to his request to appoint him Governor of the Province of Cuyo, comprising the jurisdictions of Mendoza, San Juan and San Luis. This country was partly Chilean in character; it had been transferred in 1776 from Chile to the viceroyalty of La Plata. San Martín gave as his reason for seeking this transfer the fact that his health was bad and that the doctors said he was suffering from an

66

infected lung. He asked to be relieved of army duties and allowed to recuperate in the mild and lovely climate of Mendoza, at the foot of the Andes.

Meanwhile, there had been important developments elsewhere. In June, 1814, there had been a great victory for the patriots when Carlos Alvear took the city of Montevideo. Joy at this success was short lived, however, as civil war broke out for control of the newly captured city. On one hand the Buenos Aires government demanded the city as part of their territory. On the other hand the fierce gaucho chief Artigas claimed it as ruler of the region known as the Banda Oriental (now Uruguay), a territory whose people were ready to die for him, but who had no earthly use for Buenos Aires. The provinces of Entre Rios and Corrientes, lying west and north of the Banda Oriental, then decided that they, too, would rather follow the wild gaucho, and they joined his banner. The Buenos Aires government refused to yield them the newly captured Montevideo and civil war broke out, with the result that thousands of soldiers were diverted to it who might otherwise have been fighting the Goths.

In spite of this misfortune, however, the fall of Montevideo was a milestone in the revolution. In Spain the Napoleonic war had ended with the return of Ferdinand "the Desired." Ferdinand had been planning what to do about the rebels and had decided on an invasion of the Viceroyalty, using Montevideo as a base. With that city's fall, however, Spain lost her foothold on the eastern seacoast. Nor could a royalist invasion from Peru succeed, for even if the royalists could fight their way through the

67

frontier, there would be no base of supplies to assist them. They realized now that it would be no easy task to subdue the patriots.

But the crown and the royalists were by no means without resources. Spain, after having been torn into fragments by the Peninsular War, was again an integrated country and could pour money, munitions and troops across the ocean. To chasten her rebel subjects, she could now dispatch seasoned veterans, experts in war, trained by years of grueling battle against Napoleon's forces. When these powers were assembled against the rebels, the fighting would be desperate.

In 1814 also it became apparent to the Argentinians that their mountain campaign in Peru was a failure, and that some other method must be found to secure victory.

Above all, the year 1814 marked the ascendancy of José de San Martín as the dominating personality of the revolution. His plan for victory, matured in Mendoza, was clear, concise and brilliant; it was to save the future of the new world.

Chapter IX

O RARE MENDOZA!

SAN MARTÍN rode into the place where, as Governor of Cuyo Province, he was to organize the Army of the Andes and to spend the happiest days of his life. Mendoza was only a small town, but it possessed then, as it does today, a character all its own, and it holds a high place in the historical annals of Argentina. It lies among fertile vineyards at the foot of the giant Andes ranges. In those primitive days, coming upon it after the dreary, exhausting journey over the pampas was like stumbling on an oasis, so delightful was this richly irrigated country with its long lines of canals bordered by graceful poplars. It was a land of plenty, the centre of the trans-Andean trade; the inhabitants, proud of their orchards and gardens, were most hospitable to the stranger.

The British traveler, Samuel Haigh, who visited there in San Martín's time, described the little city: "Were I to live to the age of a pelican, I could never forget sweet Mendoza; whether it be the air, the inhabitants, or the country around, or all of these combined, I know not, but there is an indelible charm attached to that spot, which I shall retain 'whilst memory holds its seat.' I have since revisited this rurality twice, and never left it without reluctance and regret." And San Martín felt likewise. Through all the vicissitudes of his stormy life, Mendoza, which today treasures so many of his relics, remained his favorite spot. His spirit still haunts its poplar-shaded streets, and each generation of Mendozans thrills at his story.

When he was settled, he sent for his girl-wife Remedios, who was then eighteen years old. As a farewell present her father gave her a black slave, Jesusa, and they were accompanied by some Mendoza friends; a relative of Remedios, Encarnacion Escalada de Lawson, acted as a chaperon. Those were the covered wagon days of Argentina. It was a trying trip at best in the springless high-wheeled wagon drawn by oxen over the desolate pampas, that "sea of land," stretching for a thousand miles, thick with marshes, continually swept by fierce winds. Scattered here and there were a few miserable huts with an equally miserable inn, before which often lay the remains of some overridden, tortured horse which had dropped as shelter was attained. The traveler caught glimpses of stray wild swans, hare, deer, and bands of ostriches, which the gauchos called "mirth of the desert." Sometimes a gaucho, wrapped in a poncho, his bare feet thrust into heavy stirrups, rode by. He fingered the silver knife in his sash, eyeing the strangers with suspicion. Or the traveler saw him flash by in pursuit of the fleeing ostriches, swinging his lasso with the stone *boleadora* as he went. A more comfortable encounter was to meet the frequent long convoys of mules, in double or triple file, carrying the sweet wine of Mendoza down to Buenos Aires.

In good weather, the trip from Buenos Aires to Mendoza took over three weeks and the wayfarer had to be prepared for any adventure. To cheer the long hours, the lusty postilions sang merry ballads as the cart creaked along.

Little Remedios set up housekeeping in Mendoza and brought with her the hospitable spirit of her father's home. Her happy, frank nature made friends for her at once. With some of the young ladies at Mendoza, she embroidered a standard known as the banner of the Andes that was later carried to the conquest of Chile and Peru. Her husband, with his usual lack of interest in personal gain, lived on half his pay as governor, donating the other half to the cause, while every ounce of his energy was devoted to developing the details of his great plan.

Although it was nothing more than a cottage, their small house was a pleasant centre where the young Argentine officers made the acquaintance of the Mendoza señoritas. The San Martíns caught the popular fancy. The new governor's exquisite tact never wounded anyone's *amour propre*, for he spoke to each man in his own language. General Gerónimo Espejo, who made the Andean campaign with him, left an interesting account of these days. Everyone had blind faith in the patriot cause and in their commander. His magnificent horsemanship was admired by the citizens who rode almost before they walked; the soldiers, whom he called his *muchachos*, adored him and took him their troubles. "That extraordinary power of dominating men," wrote Espejo, "seemed to have bewitched the people of Mendoza." Never again was San Martín so genial, so optimistic as when, his great ideal constantly in mind, he ruled in this simple democracy.

He governed like an old-time patriarch. One day a

71

farmer woman was brought before him, accused of defaming the patriots.

"So she is a farm owner and abuses the fatherland! Let her pay a fine of ten dozen squashes for the ranch of the country's soldiers."

He had forbidden any officer to enter the munition laboratory wearing military boots or spurs, for fear that a spark struck by the iron might cause an explosion. A sentinel was stationed at the door to enforce this order. One day San Martín himself appeared wearing both boots and spurs.

"You cannot pass, my General."

"But I was the one who gave the order, so I can revoke it."

"Up to now the order stands, my General."

The next day the scene was repeated, but the sentinel was adamant and refused to let him pass. San Martín returned wearing a pair of sandals and was allowed to enter. The sentinel was summoned to the General's office.

"I have brought you here to extend my congratulations. Rather than see his orders disobeyed, a good sentinel should let himself be killed, no matter who tries to set those orders aside."

And, shaking hands with the man, San Martín gave him an ounce of gold.

On another occasion an officer, seemingly in great distress, called on him. Ushered into his presence, the officer said, "I have asked to speak to San Martín, the citizen, not to San Martín, the general."

"You are speaking with the citizen," replied the chief.

"I wish to confide to you a secret that concerns my

72

TRAVELING WAGON IN A (PONTANO) MORASS

honor," said the officer, explaining that so great was his passion for gambling that he had lost a sum of money which he had taken out of his regiment's treasury.

The General rose, took from his purse the amount the officer had mentioned and gave it to him gravely. "Here, return this to the treasury," he said, "and be careful to guard this secret that you have confided to Citizen San Martín, because if it ever came to the ears of General San Martín, he would order you to be shot."

He wrote in April, 1815, "I cannot express the degree of gratitude which binds me to this people of Mendoza." Without them, there would have been no Army of the Andes to break the grip of Spain.

Chapter X

THE ARMY OF THE ANDES IS BORN

IN 1814 the Viceroy of Peru had sent General Mariano
Osorio and a large force to Chile to subdue that rebellious province. The patriots, under Bernardo O'Higgins, put up a desperate fight, but were decisively defeated
at Rancagua in October, and the Spanish crown re-established the colonial government there. In spite of the snow
that still covered the Andes at that season, hundreds of
refugees, military and civilian, poured over the mountains
into Mendoza, horrifying the people with tales of Spanish
atrocities.

War spirit flamed in the little town and the citizens
hardly stopped work to sleep or eat. As one man they set
about creating an army. Such community co-operation had
never before been known in Argentina. Even the drivers
of carts bringing munitions from Buenos Aires would accept no pay for the trip. The laborers sowed part of their
fields for the soldiers or shared their crops with San Martín, who supervised and directed every detail of the building of the Army of the Andes. Never had a leader enjoyed
deeper loyalty. The whole province was divided into workers and fighting men, the army being maintained partly by
voluntary subscription, partly by levy of a tax. Mules,
horses and equipment were lent until the war was over, and
regiment horses were pastured free of charge on the pro-

74

prietors' estates. The women wove and dyed the cloth for thousands of blue uniforms for their men who were to battle for American independence.

There came one day to the town council a delegation of ladies armed with packages; at the head was little Doña Remedios, who in a shaking voice delivered her first public speech: "Señores, we fully realize the dangers threatening the beings most dear to us, the lack of capital, the magnitude of the sacrifices necessary to preserve their liberty. We feel that diamonds and pearls are unsuitable in the serious situation of the province; still less fitting would they be, if through defeat the chains of a new serfdom should be imposed upon us. For these reasons, we prefer to sacrifice them on the altars of our country with the earnest desire of contributing towards the triumph of the Argentinians' sacred cause."

As the embarrassed girl finished she unwrapped her bundle on the table, and the other ladies did likewise. There lay necklaces, bracelets and earrings of diamonds, sapphires, and emeralds, heirlooms handed down from the conquistadores or gifts symbolizing the prosperity of the Creole landowners. They had stripped themselves cheerfully of their greatest treasures.

In June, 1815, San Martín heard through refugees from the oppressive Spanish government in Chile that General Osorio was planning to attack the Province of Cuyo when the warm weather set in. Delegating his command temporarily to a subordinate, he spent two months riding through the cordilleras and the territory to the south, studying the roads through the passes. He returned from the trip so ill that a consultation of physicians was summoned. It was the worst calamity that could have happened. He sent a plea to Buenos Aires: "These men [the physicians] are of the unanimous opinion that my life can not be prolonged more than a year, unless I immediately change my tempo of living and lead a tranquil existence until recovery. Even without this advice, I am convinced of this truth; inasmuch, for the last three months, in order to obtain a little sleep, I have had to be seated in a chair, and as the repeated attacks of vomiting blood are supremely debilitating, therefore I ask a four months' leave of absence to rest, either in the Valley of Catamarca or the Sierras of Cordoba, those being the localities I already know and would prefer."

He felt if he could only get himself in good health again, the war work would proceed efficiently. For now progress was slow. His task was to raise, equip and train an army to cross the Andes, and fight through to victory; but he had no supplies and no money; the Argentine government was always polite, but quite deaf to his appeals for help.

In November, 1815, came bad news. The third and last Argentinian attempt to invade the north had met with terrible disaster at Sipe-Sipe in Upper Peru. To San Martín it meant burning his bridges behind him. It was clearly impossible to invade Peru by land. Over the Andes alone lay the last desperate chance to win the War of Independence. Ill as he was, he gave a banquet immediately after the report of this latest disaster, and rising from his seat with a flushed face, he offered with trembling voice this toast to the officers: "To the first shot fired across the Andes against the oppressors of Chile."

His constant insomnia grew so serious, and the pains that

76

racked his body were so unremitting, that his physician gave him opium. In January, 1816, came another hemorrhage. Though it was diagnosed as lung hemorrhage, it was probably from a gastric ulcer. Excusing his delay in correspondence, he wrote to Godoy Cruz: "A violent hemorrhage, and a consequent extreme weakness have kept me prostrate in bed for nineteen days; the delays in my work as a result of these attacks keep me more and more confined to my office, while the activities of the enemy and my preparations to receive him in case of invasion, have caused me to forget my friends. All these circumstances claim your indulgence."

Night and day the fear tormented him that he might die before he could free his countrymen. His plan was no longer a vision. Though he lay ill and exhausted, the details of the campaign grew more definite. He realized that he was the only leader with the logic of mind and the tenacity of will to carry it out with success. If he died, American freedom would remain a dream.

By 1816 the Government of the United Provinces of Argentina had come to realize that their people, surrounded by perils on all sides and facing an uncertain future, needed a formal and definite statement of independence that would hearten and stabilize them. On July 9, in the small mountain town of Tucumán, a congress assembled for that purpose, for which thirty-two deputies were chosen by electoral assemblies based on the census of the population of each province. Delegates came from the ten provinces of the Argentine region, as well as from districts of Upper Peru then occupied by the royalists. They were all of excellent education, a large proportion being doctors

77

of law, and there were four priests noted for their intellectual attainments. The declaration of independence was merely a clarification of a condition that had existed since 1810, and the motion for framing the act, carried by enthusiastic acclamation, proclaimed the complete independence from Spain of the provinces of La Plata; the title of the new state was to be the United Provinces of South America.

Then began discussion of the future form of government. General Belgrano, before the opening, had, in a secret session, addressed the Congress on this subject. Pointing out that after the horrors of the French Revolution the sympathy of the civilized world had turned away from democratic disorder, he felt that it would be unthinkable for the new country not to recognize this trend. If the independence of Peru could be accomplished, the most feasible plan seemed to him the establishment of an Indian prince of Inca ancestry, who would reign in Cuzco, ancient capital of the Incas, as monarch of a United Peru and Argentina. If the scheme seemed too fantastic to the delegates, there were many princes abroad, most suitable and willing.

Belgrano's speech had been listened to with respectful thoughtfulness. To the conservative majority, the person of a monarch seemed an aid in unifying the country and in developing loyalty. The moderately monarchistic preferences of most of the other Argentine leaders were known to all, and the delegates began to debate on the future government in a most sympathetic mood towards the creation of a limited monarchy. On the other hand, the spirit of the Argentine masses had always been demo-

78

cratic, even in the days when they were a crown colony. Titles of nobility had been almost nonexistent, slaves had always been kindly treated, and the atmosphere of feudalism was alien to them. For nearly a decade they had felt their aloofness from monarchy, and in their *cabildo abierto* they had decided momentous issues. Freedom had grown increasingly sweet, and if the success of the revolution meant only a return to another monarchy, however constitutional, their victory would seem completely hollow. The word *independencia* was incompatible with any government savoring of the cruel past. Monarchy suggested only persecutions.

A very important leader of the democratic forces in the Congress was Dr. Añchoreña of Buenos Aires, but the most eloquent spokesman for democracy in the gathering was a Dominican monk, Fray Justo Santa Maria de Oro, a saintly scholar who came of the blood of the conquistadores. A South American Patrick Henry, he rose to face a prejudiced audience. Undisturbed, he poured out in burning words the thoughts nearest his heart. He pictured the incongruity of a monarchy on American soil. Were all the years of heartbreaking struggle to go for nothing? Were they to clip their wings, renounce the great adventure? Was the age-long vision of liberty to be realized on a new continent, or was this continent to go through the same story of human misery and oppression as the Old World. "I certainly have not come here," he concluded, "to treat of monarchical governments but to deliberate concerning the Argentine nation; therefore, Señores, I protest and I retire."

Wrapping himself in his mantle, he walked from the

79

room. In the words of Alberto Gerchunoff, "every one realized that that monk, impressive in his decision, in the sobriety of his condemnation, in his patriotic vehemence, had forever buried the monarchy and the fantastic prince who was to revive the dynasty of the Incas to be installed at Cuzco. He was the first to express in concrete word the will of the masses of the South American Continent." The cause of aristocracy was lost. No monarch was ever to rule the sturdy United Provinces. There was added to the declaration of independence from King Ferdinand VII, from his successors, and from the mother country, the phrase, "and from any other foreign domination." This was to discredit all rumors of European entanglements. The eloquence of Fray Justo had swayed the assembly to a new order.

San Martín, although too busy to attend the Congress, was delighted by the declaration of independence, which he had repeatedly urged, impressing the Argentine government with the inconsistency and lack of clarity in its position. At last the bridges had been burnt.

On August 24, 1816, his only child, a daughter, was born. She was baptized by Don Lorenzo Guiraldo, the camp chaplain, with the name of Mercedes Tomasa. The health of the young mother declined almost immediately from that time, but she entered as intensely as ever into her husband's plans. One could often see them in the late afternoon at a small open-air cafe in the Alameda, where they took ices in summer, coffee in winter, while the Mendozans gathered in groups about them, chatting over the news.

The resources of the faithful province of Cuyo were

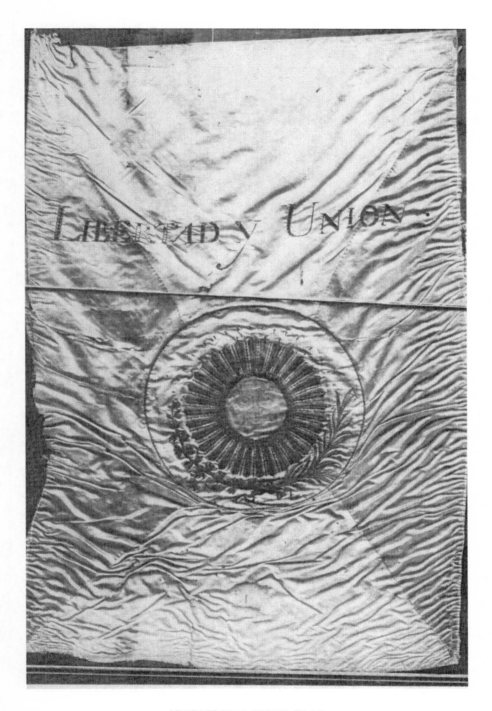

ARGENTINA'S FIRST FLAG

rapidly becoming exhausted. More than a million car-
tridges were needed, fifteen hundred horses, and more
than twelve thousand pack mules. In response to frantic
appeals, the Argentine government said it was unable to
send more funds and told him to wait until the financial
situation should improve, meaning in plain language that
it refused any more assistance.

Desperate at this final rebuff, San Martín replied, "If I
can't gather together the mules I need, I shall go on foot.
Time is lacking, money is lacking, my health is bad, but
we are aiming at the superhuman. . . . Enough said;
to advance I need thirteen hundred mules which I have to
furnish without a penny. But we are in the immortal
province of Cuyo, and everything gets accomplished.
Tongues fail, words fail to describe the stuff that these
inhabitants are made of."

Needless to say, the mules were provided. In another
letter to the Director at Buenos Aires, San Martín pays
high tribute to his devoted Mendozans.

"It is a marvel that a country moderately peopled,
without public treasury, without commerce [the trade of
Mendoza had been shattered when the royalists retook
Chile], without great capitalists, lacking wood, hides,
wool, abundant cattle and other fundamental and important articles, could raise in its midst an army of three
thousand men, depriving themselves even of the slaves,
their only means of carrying on their agricultural pursuits;
that these people could meet their debts, maintain their
living and that of a thousand refugees, promote the establishment of an arsenal, laboratories of saltpetre and powder,
an armory, park, fueling mill, barracks, training field. . . .

I need not mention the continual service of all their militia, detachments of men sent to the Cordilleras, garrisons, and many other tasks; nor the indefatigable and volunteer work of their artists in the work of the State. In short, their private fortunes almost belong to the public. The great part of the people think only of offering up their means to the common conservation.

"America is free, Excellent Sir, and her bitter enemies will tremble, dazzled by the glow of such solid virtues."

It was the American ideal that San Martín emphasized —not merely the freedom of Argentina, but the freedom of the continent. Had this ideal been cherished by other leaders, the twentieth century would have seen the United States of South America, and the bloody tale of petty local dictators and revolutions would never have been written.

An invaluable assistant to San Martín in those hectic days was a strange and picturesque Mendozan, a Franciscan friar by the name of Luis Beltran. He was a jack of all trades, and master of all. He was a trained blacksmith, a gifted mathematician, draftsman, architect and chemist; and he had a keen understanding of human beings and a tremendous sense of humor. San Martín placed him in charge of the arsenal. He made not only cannon and shot (some from the metal of church bells), but saddles for the cavalry, knapsacks and shoes for the infantry, and wagons that could carry war equipment over high Andean trails. Out of ropes and cables he made the hanging bridges so necessary to cross the mountain chasms. He was, in short, a magician. "If the cannons

82

need wings, they shall have them," said Fray Luis Beltran.

Two-thirds of the negro slaves held by wealthy Mendozans were freed voluntarily by their masters, and they formed a battalion of about seven hundred, nearly all of whom met death in the campaign. The fifty-five British residents of the city formed themselves into a corps, and a British physician, Dr. Paroissien, had charge of the medical corps and supervised the making of tents and supplies for the wounded. An expert in chemistry conducted the laboratory where gunpowder and saltpetre were turned out. One of Fray Beltran's last-minute tasks was the preparation of fifty thousand horseshoes needed for the stony Andean trails. This was a great innovation in a country where horses were never shod.

Mendoza was a town with a single thought. In a hundred subtle ways, San Martín aroused enthusiasm for the struggle, by making the townspeople feel that they were the brains and heart of the holy cause. Mendoza was the Army of the Andes; it was Mendoza which would triumph. Even the school children drilled incessantly and studied military tactics.

In Buenos Aires they were sick to death of unsuccessful war. The Argentine government looked on the Mendoza project as a madcap expedition and refused to sink any more money in patriotic ventures. It was not until Don Juan de Pueyrredon became Director of the United Provinces of La Plata that the slightest impression was made. In June, 1816, after a two-day interview at Cordoba, San Martín won him over; during his three years of office, he steadily supported the latter, supplying saddles, tents and

83

arms. On December 21, 1816, Pueyrredon signed the instructions for the expedition, which had for its object first the freeing of Chile, ultimately the complete independence of South America from Spain. The Director disclaimed all ambition to conquer any territory for Argentina. San Martín was to forbid his soldiers to plunder; if the campaign was successful, he was to arrange for a provisional government for Chile, in the hope that Chile would enter into a permanent alliance with Argentina as an independent nation.

Through all the endless planning with its thousands of details, San Martín was without confidants or counsellors; he was sole guide, judge and director. He sent Remedios and the baby back to her family in Buenos Aires and did not see her again for two years, as the campaigns absorbed him utterly. Apparently she never questioned the decision, but meekly did as she was told. It was hardly enough compensation for her singularly childlike, clinging nature to be the wife of the country's greatest patriot, worshiping from afar as he went about his superhuman task. She treasured his rare letters and waited sadly in her parents' great house in the capital. In those days women without men, whatever their status, led a life of Oriental seclusion if they wished to avoid scandal. While San Martín mapped his plans to free a continent, Remedios' life at best was very dreary.

In those Mendoza days he wore the dark uniform of the mounted Grenadiers, with high riding boots and the typical oilskin hat. His life was austere, Spartan; rising with the dawn, he worked all morning in the office, giving audiences to all who sought them, attending to ceaseless details. At noon he would select food from the kitchen, generally a puchero stew or a dish of roast meat, often eating it standing. Two glasses of the wine for which Mendoza is famous completed his repast. In summer he would then take a siesta on his favorite sheepskin; in winter he would take a walk, smoking his black tobacco cigarette. He would prepare coffee for himself, then get back to work again, inspecting public buildings and preparations in camp. At night, before he retired at ten, he received social calls, but no discussion of politics was allowed. His favorite game was chess, and it is no wonder that he was an expert, for he had the chess player's mind. He planned his battles like chess games, and he foresaw and forestalled every possible move of the enemy.

All kinds of rumors were afloat about him. "Severe in discipline, honorable, austere, and disinterested." Thus ran a confidential Spanish report at the time. And "he had a genius for austere patience and orderly procedure." Other reports throughout Argentina were not so flattering. He was a spy in the pay of Spain. What sane man would have thrown away his high position in the Spanish army? He was a drunkard, a glutton; he was plotting to make himself a monarch. This latter report grew and grew with the years. Gossip never bothered San Martín much. Commenting on these rumors in a letter to Godoy Cruz, he quoted Epictetus, "If the evil that is spoken of thee be true, correct it. If it be a lie, laugh." This very serene indifference irritated the vulgar political mind and only increased the venom of his enemies.

One of his letters to Col. Tomas Guido, however,

showed that sometimes malice did get under his skin. When affairs were at a standstill in 1816, he wrote:

"What do you wish me to say concerning the expedition to Chile? No matter when it is undertaken, the hour is late. Believe me, my friend, that I was convinced it would not come to pass, solely because I was at the head of things. Accursed be my star which only inspires a lack of confidence. Ah, friend, what miserable creatures are we animals who have two feet and no wings."

In spite of discouragement, however, San Martín was preparing the ground for the invasion of Chile by introducing a new form of strategy known as "Guerra de Zapa" or "Fox Warfare." General Osorio's persecution of the patriots residing in Chile caused them to lend a willing ear to Argentine overtures. Each side had its busy Fifth Column. A Spanish friar captured in Mendoza had documents for royalist sympathizers concealed in his hood. These Spaniards were arrested, given the papers and forced to send replies to the Spanish General; the replies, dictated by San Martín, gave the enemy completely false information concerning the preparations in Mendoza. One Pedro Vargas, an ardent patriot of the town, was of great assistance. San Martín announced that Vargas was a traitor in league with the Goths across the mountains and ordered him incarcerated. So well did Vargas play his part that his patriotic wife threatened to divorce him for his disloyalty. Passing as a victim of San Martín's tyranny, he was enabled to secure much useful information from the Spaniards who were his jailmates. When Osorio was replaced by Marco del Pont, the task was easier. From San Martín's acquaintance with del Pont in campaign days in Spain, he knew him to be childishly irritable and intensely vain, a politician who owed his advancement to sycophancy. His stupidity laid him open to Fox Warfare and San Martín's Fifth Columnists continually came and went over the Andes, reporting the royalists' plan of defense and pointing out the enemy's weak spots.

The most daring spy of all was Manuel Rodríguez, formerly Carrera's secretary, now a lawyer. As a revolutionary agent, he traversed the central provinces and cities of Chile, interviewing prominent citizens who were rumored to be friendly, secretly organizing armed bands, constantly crossing the treacherous mountain passes in every kind of weather. A high price was placed on his head, but although he worked more than a year in Chile, he was never caught. So great was his personal popularity that not one among his wide circle of acquaintances could be induced to betray him.

A mounted Grenadier, Aldao by name, was sent over the Andes to see if it were possible to transport a large army through the passes. His report was very favorable; so wily San Martín gave out that an invasion of Chile through the Los Patos and Uspallata passes (respectively north and south of Mt. Aconcagua, highest peak in the western hemisphere) would be hopeless and that the attack would have to be made by way of the south. Del Pont's Fifth Columnists reported this announcement to him, causing him to withdraw men from the north and strengthen his defenses in southern Chile. Professor William Spence Robertson says, "The student of history will search long in military annals to find a campaign more carefully matured, more systematically prepared for, and more successfully executed than his [San Martín's] march over the Andean range."

In San Martín's account books of the time are found significant receipts:

Received from Señor General-in-Chief six ounces of gold for a secret commission.

MENDOZA, October 23, 1815
Francisco Lino de Villota

I, the undersigned, affirm that I have received from the Señor General-in-Chief Don José de San Martin, the sum of one hundred eighty-three pesos in current money for very secret expenses on behalf of the patria, and therefore I set hereto my signature this fourth of September, 1816.

PEDRO VARGAS

The following letter, supposedly written by a Spanish sympathizer in Mendoza, is typical of the correspondence that was manufactured to fall into the hands of the Captain General of Chile.

"The despair that has overcome these people, and on the other hand the reckless character of their leader is causing them to make efforts beyond their power. Invaded by a formidable Portuguese expedition which landed in Maldonado on the thirtieth of last month and which is continuing its marches in order to lay siege to Montevideo, and the so-called army of Peru having retreated to Tucumán, they feel that nothing possible remains but to make an attempt on Chile. They have marched by way of the province of Concepcion. The plan is to send one thousand men by one of the roads of the south. . . . Santa Fe is in rebellion against Buenos Aires, and the latter's men are beaten."

Countless forged letters were sent to Chile, belittling the number of troops at Mendoza as well as their morale. One note relates that San Martín's officers were in despair about the invasion plans, but that the "stubborn and violent character" of their chief brooked no opposition to the "nonsensical scheme."

The climax to his Fox Warfare came when San Martín sent invitations to the chiefs of the Pehenches Indians, an Araucanian tribe inhabiting the eastern slope of the Andes, asking them to confer with him at the fortress of San Carlos, south of Mendoza, for the purpose of concluding a pact of alliance. He took with him gifts of horse gear, cloth and glass beads for the women, and much Mendoza sweet wine and aguardiente. A month later the Indians paid him a return visit in Mendoza. San Martín had them witness the army performing its maneuvers, and was amused at their terror of the "noisy magic" coming out of the cannons. When they sat down on the ground for the eagerly awaited feast, San Martín, sitting among them, gravely remarked, "I must tell you that I have heard that the Spaniards plan to come over from Chile to kill you all and steal your wives and your children.

"But," he went on, as the Indians stared at him in terror, "that I shall never permit, and as I also am an Indian, I am going to destroy these Goths who have taken this country from your ancestors. To do this I intend to cross the Andes with the cannons you have just heard. I intend to cross through South Chile and for that I need your permission as you are the owners of that land."

They solemnly gave their consent and then, falling on food and drink, started a debauch which lasted eight days.

Naturally the news soon drifted over to Chile, via the talkative chiefs, that an alliance had been concluded between the Indians and the patriots, that the Indians were to furnish cattle and horses, and that the Army of the Andes was to march into Southern Chile.

One thing more needed to be done before the Army of the Andes could march. There was no detailed map of the passes of Uspallata and Los Patos through which they would traverse the mountains. San Martín had a happy idea. There was a Major José Antonio Alvarez de Condarco, an engineer gifted with a stupendous memory. The General ordered him to cross over to Chile by the Los Patos road, to study it intensely and, without making a single note, to bring back a map of the route in his head. He was to carry with him a copy of the recently promulgated Declaration of Argentine Independence. If the Spanish captain general, who was of most uncertain temper, did not order Condarco shot, he was to return to Argentina by the shorter pass of Uspallata, observing every rock on the road.

Condarco executed his dangerous mission with brilliant success. He nearly met his death at the hands of the Spanish leaders who, however, decided to burn the Declaration of Independence in the public square in Santiago and send San Martín a furious reply by Condarco, who on his return executed accurately from memory a complete map of both passes.

As San Martín had written, "We are in the immortal province of Cuyo, and everything gets accomplished."

90

Chapter XI

OVER THE ANDES LIES CHILE

THE JANUARY summer had come and the time was ripe to march. San Martín settled his army on the Plumerillo, an open plain to the north of Mendoza, for the finishing touches. The men were divided into three divisions, commanded respectively by Colonel Gregorio de Las Heras, General Miguel Soler and General Bernardo O'Higgins. General Soler was to take the vanguard by the pass of Los Patos, winding around the north side of Mt. Aconcagua. O'Higgins with the reserve was to follow, while Las Heras, with a small body of infantry and artillery, was to go through the Uspallata Pass south of Aconcagua. Each commander had from San Martín an itinerary of the march, with minute instructions and maps of the routes. The plan was for the forces to unite after crossing the Andes; arriving on the plain, they were to defeat the enemy and capture Santiago. It has been said that the campaign was planned on San Martín's pillow. Days before it was fought, his chess player's mind had planned it to the minutest detail and forestalled any possible counterattack by the Goths.

He wrote to a friend that conquering the Goths did not worry him half so much as getting his men over the tremendous mountains. For their food they were to carry dried roasted beef, ground finely and thickly mixed with fat, garlic and onions, which were an aid against mountain sickness. Rope bridges were woven to throw over the abysses. Remembering that in places the passes were so narrow that only single horsemen could traverse them, San Martín sent groups of workmen ahead to clear the way.

In 1817 the Andes were passable only through the two passes of Los Patos and Uspallata, both of them over thirteen thousand feet high—and then only in summer. Even today, when planes make the trip in one hour from Santiago to Mendoza, droning from eighteen to twenty thousand feet in the air past Aconcagua, second in height only to Mt. Everest, the crossing is not to be undertaken lightly, and passengers are taken over only in good weather. In 1817, crossing these mountains was perilous at every step of the slippery path. "Condors wheeling in airy circles at dizzy heights are the only living things seen. Below roar the mountain streams, carrying great rocks, tossing them about as they would toss straws. Here only stunted cacti, mosses and thorny plants exist. The world is seen as it emerged from chaos in the process of creation." Such, in the words of the historian, Dr. Bartolomé Mitre, were the obstacles before the Army of the Andes.

On January 17, 1817, they were to leave Mendoza. The city held a fiesta and the streets were strewn with flowers. Tapestries of colonial times hung from the windows, and men and women wore gala costumes. The army entered the plaza where a platform had been erected. San Martín ascended it carrying the flag embroidered by Remedios and the Mendoza ladies. He himself had selected the fabrics, blue and white, and had been most particular about the shade of blue, which finally had been secured from a street peddler. On the flag was a shield with a rising sun and two hands lifting a red liberty cap over mountain crests. It had first been blessed in the church where the Army had been dedicated to its patroness, Our Lady of Carmen. Baring his head, San Martín unfurled the banner to the cheering crowds. "This is the first independent flag to be blessed in America, soldiers. Swear to protect it and die in its defense!"

"We swear it," shouted ten thousand voices, as the people roared their *vivas* and every church bell rang out. It was Mendoza's great day in history.

Everything succeeded. On January 18, Las Heras' division left the town, carrying carts and cables to aid the transportation of cannon. San Martín, in his Grenadier's uniform and mounted on a mule, departed a few days later for the Uspallata Pass. Leaving behind the pleasant vineyards of the Mendoza country, he rode through a barren desolate region up towards the cordilleras, sharp, jagged, black peaks covered with perpetual snow. As he climbed, a terrible hailstorm forced him to descend from his mule and wait for its passing. The cold was intense on the heights, six degrees below zero. Farther up in the mountains the soldiers were caught by the storm, but their band defiantly played the new national hymn of Argentina. "The cordillera," they said, "is indignant at having on it for the first time the tread of warriors."

It was a splendid piece of strategy for San Martín to have deceived the Captain General of Chile about his march, for success would have been out of the question had the passes of Los Patos and Uspallata been guarded.

93

The day fixed for the three divisions to reunite after passing the Andes was February 8, and on February 8, so it came to pass. Three weeks after their departure from Mendoza, after one of the most terrible marches in history, the soldiers of Soler, O'Higgins and Las Heras had, with some losses, passed the Andes and were encamped in the foothills. San Martín wrote home his report to Director Pueyrredon:

"The passage of the Andes has been a triumph in itself. The soldiers of the army with supplies for almost a month, with armament, munitions of war, and baggage have marched a hundred leagues along a road which crossed craggy peaks, defiles, fords, and deep, narrow chasms—a road intersected by four mountain ridges, where the cragginess of the soil competes with the asperity of the atmosphere. If to overcome these obstacles has been to gain a victory, it is no less a victory because it has frightened the enemy."

With the exception of the Himalayas, the Andes are the highest mountains ever traversed by an army. It was a feat unparalleled in military annals, more spectacular than the marches of Alexander, Hannibal or Napoleon.

There was need for quick action. The Spanish Colonel Alero had sent a body of men to Uspallata Pass to study the ground about the time that General Las Heras and his division were marching through. Las Heras' vanguard came face to face with them, chased them out of the pass. They fled to General Marco del Pont and spread the alarm of the invasion. San Martín, hearing this, saw he must strike before the royalists could unite their forces.

94

A night attack was decided on to catch the enemy off his guard.

Near Santiago is the plain of Chacabuco where the Spanish forces had encamped; the plan was to attack simultaneously on their vanguard and flank, thereby cutting off their retreat to Santiago. At midnight San Martín's men descended into the plain; it was moonlight and the giant Andes, unearthly white, stood out like spirit mountains. Below them shone the lights of the encamped Goths, who were still in a panic over the news of the unexpected invasion. They were without a commander until February 11, when General Rafael Maroto, a man ignorant of the country, arrived and hysterically tried to draw up a plan of battle.

As his men filed silently down to the plain, San Martín watched them from the heights. A terrible rheumatic attack had so crippled him that he could hardly sit his horse, although long before the end of the battle he dashed down into the conflict.

Bernardo O'Higgins, without awaiting orders and rashly forgetting instructions, charged on the enemy lines with a division of only one thousand men. San Martín's keen eyes saw that this recklessness would lose the battle, for the Spanish cavalry could easily smash O'Higgins' small detachment. Placing himself at the head of three squadrons of Grenadiers, he charged down on the enemy cavalry and beat them back, saving O'Higgins. He had ordered General Soler's division to advance at the same time. The rapidly executed march of the Argentine army gave the royalist commander no time to protect the fleeing vanguard; he became utterly confused and fled, pursued by the Grenadiers. The battle turned into a wild rout, and the road to Santiago lay open.

The Goths had been deserted by their leader, but many of their divisions held and fought desperately until nightfall. It had been a savage fight. Among the Spanish dead lay many with their heads severed from their bodies by sabre cuts. The Grenadiers had not forgotten San Martín's famous saying, "If a Goth stands in your way, sever his head like a watermelon." Victory was theirs and nothing had failed. A funeral pyre shot its flames to the skies as the corpses were burned on the field, and a message went forth from San Martín to the faithful province of Cuyo.

"Let admirable Cuyo glory in the fact that the object of its sacrifices has been accomplished. Chile is ours."

With his usual dread of public acclamation, the hero entered Santiago incognito, though his presence was soon discovered and the Chileans went wild over him. Captain General Marco del Pont was arrested and conducted before San Martín, who extended his right hand, saying, "Señor General, put forward that white hand of yours." This had reference to the fact that years before, del Pont, on receiving a letter from him had remarked, "I sign with a white hand, not like San Martín, whose hand is black." There had been a rumor current that the patriot leader was an Indian or at any rate a mestizo.

The officers held a banquet that night at Santiago, in the captain general's former palace, a vivid contrast to their bleak Andean camp. The Argentine national hymn was sung, and the epicurean meal was served by lovely Chilean girls dressed in Argentine colors, and wearing

SAN MARTIN IN THE ANDES

the red Phrygian caps of liberty. San Martín rose and offered a toast "to the liberty of America," smashing the glass as the company eagerly responded. Although his impassive face showed little emotion, it was probably the happiest day of his life. Brilliant success had crowned the first part of his task, and in after years it was to be a consoling memory.

When the news reached Buenos Aires, the city gave itself up to mad celebration. Cannon were fired from the ships in the river and from the fortresses; the government appointed San Martín brigadier general. In Santiago the *cabildo abierto* elected him Director of Chile. Both these honors were declined, the Chilean post because he wished to remain with the Army of the Andes and carry out his plan of going on to conquer Peru, sweeping the Goths off the continent. General O'Higgins was accordingly elected Supreme Dictator of Chile—to San Martín's delight, as the two friends worked in perfect harmony. The power behind the throne in Chile was the Lautaro Lodge, with a membership, half Chilean and half Argentinian, who made the political decisions on important questions and passed them on to O'Higgins. A decree for the coinage of money was issued, and the official declaration of Chilean independence was signed January 1, 1818, by Director O'Higgins and his three ministers. Chile was a free country.

Notwithstanding this victory, they were not out of the woods. Due to excessive prudence, San Martín committed a grave error in not following up the royalist fugitives who had fled towards the south. Not wishing to drive his tired men, already loaded down with prisoners, he allowed the enemy to go their way. Disorganized as they were by defeat, they could easily have been driven out of the country had the patriots attacked. Instead, San Martín, his one-track mind absorbed in the subjugation of Peru, busied himself with plans to finance the Lima expedition, and for that purpose undertook a lengthy trip to Buenos Aires, leaving the dispersion of the royalists to Colonel Las Heras. Las Heras tried to take Talcahuano, the fort to which they had retreated, but failed, for by that time the enemy had been reinforced by three thousand men from the Viceroy of Peru. Thus augmented, they won several minor successes and marched north on Santiago. Things began to look black for the patriot government, and San Martín rushed to the rescue.

Royalists and patriots met in a fierce battle on the plains of Concharrayada, the patriots being taken by surprise and suffering heavy losses. Las Heras retreated towards Santiago with the greater part of his troops, but all sorts of rumors preceded him. Panic was in the air. Monteagudo, the auditor general of the army, completely unnerved, galloped through the town announcing there had been a terrible rout, and the people of Santiago were in a hysteria of fear. As the vanguard of the refugees straggled in, the wildest rumors circulated. O'Higgins was mortally wounded. The Spanish conquerors were on their way to punish the rebel city; one man claimed to have seen San Martín shoot himself on the field. Prominent patriot citizens packed their families and belongings on mules and fled towards the Andes. The rank and file of the people, really indifferent to the new cause of the *patria*, made haste to climb on the bandwagon, and once again the old cry of *"Viva el Rey"* resounded through the streets. One Spanish sympathizer even had his horse shod with silver, so the Gothic commander could ride him in the triumphal parade.

Then riders brought better news, and no one knew what to believe. A despatch came from San Martín showing that, at any rate, he was alive. Next morning, with the arrival of Bernardo O'Higgins, came definite reports. In spite of the defeat, the army was still intact, except for five hundred deserters. Finally San Martín, haggard and exhausted but calm as ever, drew up at the gates of the city where one of the aristocrats of Santiago, Paula de Jara Quemada, with her children and fifty of her peons about her, stood waiting to do him homage and assure him of her loyal support. When he told her the army would have to be reorganized, she offered him her estate as a military camp.

Pushing on into the city as the bells of Santiago rang out a relieved welcome, he was surrounded by citizens who clamored for news. Standing before the great door of the palace, he rallied the people in a simple, earnest talk that re-established their confidence. "Don't be alarmed; the fatherland still exists, and it will win in the end." He spoke like a father quieting frightened children; his very aloofness increased his power over them. Quietly they returned to their homes, confident that he would save them. The following day they brought their plate and jewels in cartloads to the palace to help re-equip the army.

When Las Heras' troops rejoined San Martín's troops in the city, it was decided to set up camp on the plains of Maipú, seven miles south of Santiago, there to await the

99

enemy. Notwithstanding their victory, the royalists had been too disorganized to take advantage of their success and had followed after the patriots in a confident but most leisurely manner. What was their surprise, on fording the Maipú river with the intent to cross and capture Santiago, to find the way barred by San Martín's army drawn up in complete order, defending the city. The royalist pace had been too slow.

Chapter XII

THE BLOODY PLAIN OF MAIPÚ

O N THE plain of Maipú, seven miles southeast of Santiago, the two armies faced each other. Notwithstanding their smashing victory at Concharrayada,
the Goths, with their exhausted cavalry, were in no condition to win another battle. Their food supply was short,
and as the irrigation ditches had been cut by the patriot
army, the roads were almost impassable. Realizing they
were in a dangerous trap, they decided to attack the following day and risk all on the fight.

West of the plain of Maipú, ranges of low-lying hills
run in monotonous lines along the horizon, with patches
of high, thorny, brown bushes breaking the grey uni-
formity. The patriot army was encamped on the tableland
of the hill known as *Loma Blanca*; the Spaniards were
drawn up on two hills directly opposite. San Martín, in
his position east of the *Loma Blanca*, held command of
three roads which led into the plain of Maipú, controlling
the way to Valparaiso, and thus securing for his army a
retreat that would still protect the vulnerable part of the
capital. Santiago must be defended at all costs. Within
the city all was hysteria, for it was realized that the fate
of Chile depended on the day's outcome.

San Martín too realized that this chess game, if lost,
would mean the end of the revolution in the south. He

had spent hours studying the field; as at Chacabuco, he had provided for every chance and had already won the battle on paper. He placed his Grenadiers at the right wing, and gave command of the reserve to Col. de la Quintana. The left wing was under Colonel Alvarado, the right under Colonel Las Heras, while General Balcarce had command of the infantry. O'Higgins was lying wounded in Santiago, and a rumor came to San Martín that his friend was dead.

In order to hold their advantageous position, San Martín ordered his men not to advance until the enemy had charged to within fifty paces of their lines. On that famous morning of April 5, they stood in their ranks, each soldier knowing exactly what he had to do. They were not to stop to retrieve their wounded, as time was of the essence. Their General told them: "This battle will decide the fate of all America, and it is preferable to suffer an honorable death on the field of honor than to meet it at the hands of our executioners." By his command, detailed orders of the plan of battle, one hundred bullets and a strong drink of aguardiente had been distributed to every man in the army. It was a beautiful still day. Survivors recounted that they had never heard the meadow larks sing so sweetly. They recalled how very blue the sky was, how fragrant the yellow broom flowers and the orange blossoms. The tale of the battle has been minutely told by the Argentine historian, Dr. Mitre, who visited the field of Maipú twice and talked to patriot veterans. His first visit to the battlegrounds was with General Las Heras, the commander of the right wing; his second inspection was in the company of Chile's most distinguished his-

torians, Barros Arana and Vicuña MacKenna, and their
guide was a ninety-year old man who at seventeen had
fought the good fight that famous April day.

San Martín, dressed in a poncho and wearing a peasant
hat, saw through a field glass that the royalists were
executing a flank march to take possession of the triangular group of hills opposite the patriot army, thus prolong-
ing their angle on the Valparaiso road.

"How stupid these Goths are," he cried. "Osorio is
more of a fool than I had supposed. We are going to win.
See, the sun is our witness." It was at that moment that
the first rose and gold light of dawn streamed across the
white mountain tops. The sun was rising on the plain of
Maipú.

Hours went by and still no battle. The suspense was
terrible for the tense men. At ten-thirty San Martín
ordered them forward; at noon the armies were separated
only by a narrow ravine; it was then that he noticed the
weak flank of the royalists and ordered his reserve to attack them. Colonel de Quintana crossed the ravine, effect-
ing an oblique march on the enemy and arrived at the
east angle of the Spanish position. The battle wavering
back and forth now centered on the triangular mesa of
the Espejo hill, where the fate of South America was to
be decided. The Mounted Hunters of the Andes and the
Lancers of Chile charged forward to attack the Gothic
cavalry on the enemy's right wing. It was a magnificent
charge, magnificently resisted, a titanic struggle. The
Spanish soldier has few equals in the whirlwind of a hand-
to-hand conflict, as both Napoleon in the nineteenth century and Franco in the twentieth found to their cost. He

is an individual fighter to whom death means nothing. Creole and Spaniard, brothers in blood, hacked with sabres at one another's throats; the *mestizo*, the negro and the *zambo* followed them blindly. The cavalry on both sides literally cut each other to pieces, leaving victory to be snatched by the infantry.

The three battalions of reservists climbing the hill were meeting stiff resistance from Ordoñez, a fine Spanish leader whom San Martín had known well in the Peninsular campaigns. The famous Burgos regiment of the royalists stood gallantly against the infantry charge; they had won great distinction in Spain as a star regiment and could boast that after eighteen battles they did not know defeat. After the victory of Bailen in Spain, their flag had been crowned with a laurel wreath, and they were the most distinguished fighters of all the veterans who had faced Napoleon. These men disputed every inch, clashing against the bayonets of the infantry. It was the most crucial moment of the war. Observers could make nothing of it, because of the dust clouds and black smoke, and the hoarse cries of *"Viva el Rey"* and *"Viva la patria"* seemed equally strong.

At this point the chief Spanish commander, General Osorio, turned and fled; his best officer, Ordoñez, still tried to hold his infantry, but the narrow base on which they held their position gave them no room to maneuver and they became hopelessly confused. A bayonet charge, under San Martín, hurled itself forward and fell on the weak right flank of the enemy. The royalists, their cavalry gone, wavered but still did not break. Their last hope, the reserve of Grenadiers, separated from the left wing,

GENERAL BERNARDO O'HIGGINS

could not come to their assistance. Las Heras, the patriot general, pounded on and on against them, until they finally turned and broke into flight.

The Burgos regiment still struggled against their first defeat; they rallied again at the nearby hacienda of Espejo and fought on until the late afternoon, when they surrendered their famous banner. The battle had been won, and two thousand corpses were left on the field. Twenty-two hundred prisoners were taken. An English traveler, Samuel Haigh, was an eyewitness. He writes that some officers, veterans of years of European campaigns, told him they had never seen so bloody a combat. It had won the independence of Chile for all time, and beyond lay open the road to Peru.

San Martín, not stopping to wash the blood from his hands, dictated the news of victory from horseback. O'Higgins rose from his sickbed in Santiago and, still feverish from his wounds, galloped like a madman to the battlefield to fling his arms around San Martín's neck. "Glory, glory to the savior of Chile!" shouted the frantic Irishman.

The battle, so far-reaching in its consequences, had been won fifteen days after a crushing defeat. It broke the nerve of the Spanish government in the new world and made them realize the peril of their position. It promised the success of the invasion of Peru, as it enabled San Martín to use Chile as a naval base for his projected attack. In a sense, all subsequent victories of the war came as a result of Maipú. Its loss would have meant the failure of the Revolution in the South. General John Miller,

San Martín's British friend, writes of the excitement in the capital:

> During the cannonade, the feelings of the inhabitants of Santiago were wound up to breathless intensity, which, on the news of victory, found vent in wild expressions of ungovernable ecstasy. People embraced each other, laughed, wept, and shrieked as if deprived of their senses. Some went literally mad, and one or two of them have never recovered their reason. One man dropped down and expired instantaneously. (*Memoirs*, Vol. I, p. 186.)

Today Maipú is a little suburb of Santiago, and on the field where the bloody struggle gave Chile her freedom, stands a monument. Inscribed are the names of the officers who fought that day, with a simple dedication in honor of those who vanquished the army that had vanquished Napoleon. It reads: "To the conquerors of the conquerors of Bailen."

It was at Bailen that San Martín had won a medal for gallantry, and the grim resistance of the Burgos regiment which he had known so well in Spain must have awakened poignant memories but probably no regrets. His life had been so completely dedicated to the achievement of American freedom that personal glory meant nothing.

Characteristically, he strode quietly into Santiago, avoiding the ovation that the jubilant crowds of Santiago were preparing. He wrote in those days, "Nothing does more honor to a General than to preserve his serenity and face perils where there is a probability of victory; but nothing disgraces his name more than the useless shedding of the blood of his fellow men." Only the consciousness of his high mission ever reconciled him to the slaughter of human beings.

The chivalry of the man was shown in an incident after Maipú. His favorite aide, O'Brien, brought him the portfolios of the Spanish General Osorio, which contained his private correspondence. San Martín perused letter after letter written by well-known Chileans after the patriots' defeat at Concharrayada; in these letters the timeservers professed their unswerving devotion to the Spanish crown. He preferred to burn the papers and let the two-faced gentlemen go unpunished. Their names were never revealed by him; yet the incident made him more introspective and solitary, more questioning of uncontrolled popular government, intensifying that dislike of the mob that had remained with him since his friend Solano had perished as its victim in Cadiz.

After Maipú, San Martín addressed a communication to Viceroy Pezuela of Peru, in which he proposed a cessation of the war and the security of the liberty of the Spanish-American people. He stated also that he had treated the three thousand soldier prisoners and the two hundred captured officers humanely, in contrast to the barbarous orders issued by Spanish commanders to slaughter all captives of war. Chile and the United Provinces of La Plata desired a liberal constitution and some kind of self-government. "To attempt to restrain by the bayonet the general course of opinion in Spanish America is like attempting to enslave nature."

His appeal fell on deaf ears. The Viceroy and his court at Lima, haughty and aloof, flatly turned down his request.

Chapter XIII

SAN MARTÍN'S DREAM COMES TRUE

THE ALLIANCE between Chile and Argentina was the first to be made between nations of the new world. Dr. Mitre says of this alliance that (1) San Martín was the soul that imparted its spirit; (2) O'Higgins was the international link, Chile's guarantor; (3) the Army of the Andes was its nerve and muscle, and (4) the Lodge was its secret mechanism. Its objects were three in number: (1) its own defense as motive; (2) control of the Pacific as its means, and (3) the freedom of South America as its end.

A traveler of today, leaving Santiago in the early morning by air, arrives in Buenos Aires at three in the afternoon. In 1818 the distance could be covered by a courier in eleven days if the weather were very favorable. Post houses were established along the route where horses were in readiness at all hours. When a traveler arrived with a tired mount, the host would ride out with a lasso, catch a horse and bring him to the inn, swiftly transferring the saddle. Little care was taken of the horses as good ones could be procured for about three dollars. This journey, which would tax a constitution of iron, was made often by San Martín, and always on muleback. He set out a few days after Maipú to secure definite financial aid at Buenos Aires for the invasion of Peru. Riding into the city, he found the crowds had heard of his coming. They lined the streets, cheering the grave man whose bronzed face was lined with fatigue; flowers were flung at him, tapestries hung from the balconies in his honor. The demonstration made him impatient and nervous because of its futility. Four of the principal poets composed extravagant eulogies, but all he could get from the Congress was a vote of thanks, a commission as brigadier general, which he declined, and a vague promise to contribute five hundred thousand pesos to the Army of the Andes, to be raised by a loan.

By the time he arrived home in Mendoza, there was nothing left of the promise. A letter arrived from Director Pueyrredon informing him with regret that after all it would be impossible to grant the loan. In clear, concise terms San Martín wrote an answer, tendering his resignation as chief of the Army of the Andes. This saved the situation. His letter, read in a large meeting of the Lautaro Lodge at Buenos Aires, threw the government into consternation. Realizing what his loss would be to the cause of independence, Director Pueyrredon begged him to reconsider. Somehow they would float the loan. San Martín consented to wait for a few weeks, but he had grown suspicious of mere words. To make the promise doubly sure, he stopped the Chilean registered mail to Buenos Aires, collected from it about three hundred thousand pesos, and gave the owners of the money drafts for the amount on the Argentine government, which had to pay. It was a highhanded, desperate measure, but it saved the expedition.

While the invasion to Peru began to take shape, San

Martín tried constantly to further friendly relations between the two new allies. Many marriages, encouraged by him, were made between his Argentine officers and daughters of Chilean families. His simple evening parties became the centre of Santiago's social life, and were given a patriotic significance. As the entertainment opened, the guests would gather in a circle to sing the Argentine national hymn. San Martín then opened the ball with a minuet, after which waltzes and contre danzas alternated with the national dances, to the accompaniment of guitars played by men of the people. The conversation ranged from discussions of the latest fashions to political gossip of the day, and the latest news from Europe. San Martín always retired early, but the parties often lasted until the dawn.

Always the soldier and the Spartan, he could never relax in gay company. He gave orders that the men should wear uniforms to his evenings, while the women were to dress as simply as possible. One evening a lovely Chilean appeared in a gorgeous ball costume, wearing a diamond necklace and long diamond earrings. The effect was dazzling, but San Martín was blind to her charms, and told her that her gown was unbefitting the times.

She gave him a saucy answer, "General, you say that because you are accustomed to the frumpy country style of Mendoza."

"Yes, I *am* accustomed to Mendoza," he answered proudly, with a contemptuous look in his piercing eyes.

Women never counted in his life or interested him. He never understood or felt at ease with them. Aloof and ascetic in temperament, he had spent the greater part of his life in camps and garrisons where women of the town offered the only feminine society. Later in Argentina, women of the fashionable class, in spite of their admiration, bewildered and bored him with their chatter and flattery. He was like a cloistered friar set down suddenly in a world of which he knew nothing.

Samuel Haigh, the British traveler, describes a ball given by San Martín in honor of his friend Commodore Bowles, whose frigate *Amphion* was anchored in the Bay of Valparaiso; all the British in Santiago attended the fiesta. The entwined flags of Argentina and Chile decorated the patio, and the rooms shone with many-colored lanterns and crystal chandeliers. The higher officers of the army and all the distinguished Chileans were among the guests.

It was the first time Samuel Haigh had seen the man he describes as the "Hannibal of the Andes." The General had only just returned from a hard muleback trip to Buenos Aires; he made a deep impression on the Englishman. "He is tall and well-formed, and his whole appearance is highly military. His countenance is very expansive; his complexion a deep olive; his hair is black, and he wore large whiskers without mustachios; his eyes are large and black, and possess a fine animation which would be remarkable under any circumstances. . . . The assembly was most brilliant, consisting of all the inhabitants of the first rank in Santiago, as well as of all the chief military officers. Hundreds were performing the mazy waltz, and general satisfaction was depicted in every face."

San Martín's introvert nature found these social assemblies an intense strain, absorbed as he was in his struggles to free a continent. Furthermore, his health was very bad; gastric pains and vomiting tormented him. He wrote to his friend Godoy Cruz, "My health is in the worst possible state. I know the remedy. It is tranquility; but my extraordinary situation makes me the unhappy victim of circumstances. I have no consoling philosophy as I see myself steadily advancing towards death and with the agonizing realization that I know it and can do nothing to prevent it."

Santiago was not *simpático;* the never-ending bickering between the Chilean factions of Bernardo O'Higgins and the quarrelsome Carrera brothers were a constant irritation to him whose clear mind saw its futility when the task before them was so tremendous. While Rome was burning, they sat fiddling. Another letter to Godoy Cruz says: "To live in this country is a continual torment to me. With all its beauty, everything is antipathetic. The men especially are of a character entirely distasteful to my ideas, and I live in continual state of vexation that corrodes my sad existence."

His enemies spread the report that he was an alcoholic, which was unfounded. Since his garrison days at Cadiz he had prided himself on being a connoisseur of Spanish wines; but he was very abstemious. The real trouble was that to relieve his physical pains he was taking frequent doses of opium. Director Pueyrredon wrote Tomas Guido of a visit paid him by San Martín in which the Director had begged him to give up the drug. He replied it was impossible, that he would die without it. Young Manuel Pueyrredon said of his own trip to Chile where he stayed at San Martín's house: "He bade me wake him at seven.

CHURCH OF SANTO DOMINGO

Then he would give me the key to his closet, and I was told to bring him a bottle of thick greenish liquor and he would swallow the contents." He could not carry on without it.

His friends entered into a conspiracy to hide these vials, but rarely could secure them. The opium quieted his excited nerves, then at the breaking point; and always awful fear haunted him that death might strike before the end of his task.

Towards the end of 1818 the two great revolutionary movements of the South American continent, the one led by Simón Bolívar and originating in Caracas, the other that of San Martín from Buenos Aires, seemed to be drawing nearer together, forcing the Spaniards into Peru. Early in 1818, Bolívar had been utterly defeated and driven back from the west by the royalist General Morrillo. As time went on, luck changed. England and the United States became interested in the patriot cause. American privateers attacked Spanish vessels in the Caribbean, thousands of British volunteers came over to fight for Bolívar. Paez of Venezuela, wild leader of the plains, led his riders to victory after victory over the Goths. The beginning of the end came when Bolívar crossed the equatorial Andes and freed Colombia by the battle of Boyacá, the Maipú of the North.

In organizing the attack on Lima, time was of the utmost importance. Peru was exhausted by her efforts to repress the revolution in Chile and would have fallen instantly had the expedition sailed at once. But the same old question of an empty treasury stared them in the face. How was the money to be raised? San Martín spent the winter in Mendoza, calculating expenses. The promised five hundred thousand pesos were slow in making their appearance; due to the good offices of the League, which always stood ready to help San Martín, two hundred thousand pesos finally arrived. The General was very ill that winter in Mendoza; the ubiquitous Samuel Haigh called at his house and found him in bed, so pale and so emaciated that but for the invalid's large, very brilliant eyes, he would not have recognized him.

The plan was for Chile and Argentina to raise a squadron to control the Pacific and advance on Lima with the allied Argentine and Chilean army. And now as chief of the navy, there enters upon the stage Thomas Lord Cochrane, the most colorful, the most able sailor of the day, who had accepted an offer of San Martín's agent in London to fight for American independence. He was probably the most able navy man since Nelson, taking tremendous chances and usually winning. His life had been checkered and adventurous. A prominent radical leader in Parliament, he had been expelled from the House of Commons for a questionable stock exchange deal. Later on he was re-elected by his constituents, but political life was too dull for him, so he took to the sea. The Spaniards knew him as *El Diablo*. A born leader of men, his rare talents were shaded by his intense egotism, his vanity, and his irascibility. He would be second to none and sooner or later his impetuous personality was bound to clash with the cool impersonality of San Martín.

At first everything went well. He was given command of the naval squadron furnished by Chile, consisting of eight war vessels and sixteen transports. On board he had a fighting force of sixteen hundred soldiers and sailors, of which one thousand were Chileans, the remainder British seamen. He lost no time getting started and his work was brilliant. In January, 1820, he had seized the important port of Valdivia in South Chile and had swept the Spanish fleet off the Pacific by capturing some, forcing others to take shelter in the Bay of Callao where they were bottled up. Thus making Chile an unchallenged seapower on the Pacific, he laid open the way to Peru.

Conditions of anarchy in Argentina still held back the expedition. Lord Cochrane became the idol of Chile, riding about the town with his dashing young wife. Affairs dragged; people were restless, at high tension, and hung on the news from Buenos Aires where the question of federalism or unitarianism was the burning issue of the day. In the capital, a strong unitarian or central government was desired. In the interior provinces the gaucho groups were distrustful of the power of Buenos Aires and wanted neither a monarchy nor a centralized republic. They called themselves federalists and intrigued for a loose type of constitution which would accord to each province a vast amount of self-government. This led, of course, to civil strife, and rule by *caudillos,* or local chiefs. In Santa Fe and Entre Rios provinces civil war broke out, and the fighting was very savage. On the pampas every kind of outrage was committed; couriers were cut off, travelers murdered, horses carried away. The capital, panic-stricken and practically isolated, was threatened by revolutionary cavalry. Rondeau, the new Director, ordered San Martín to cancel all plans for the invasion of Peru at once, and march the Army of the Andes back to Buenos

Aires to defend it against the *caudillo* chiefs of Santa Fe and Entre Rios provinces.

After a very bitter but brief inner conflict, San Martín refused to obey. It was one of the great decisions of his life, and shows his breadth of vision. Satisfied by his friend O'Higgins that Chile would support the expedition, San Martín had himself carried on a stretcher from Mendoza to Santiago—over the Andes. As Kirkpatrick says, "to throw his army into the Civil War between Buenos Aires and the provinces would have wasted it in a welter of confusion." To postpone the long-delayed invasion would be fatal, as the Goths would thereby gain time to render their position impregnable. Then the war would drag on for years. He had always had the intense conviction that his sword should be drawn only against the enemies of his country. He would never fight in an internal war, where Creole slaughtered Creole. First of all, he was an American, and as he said on several occasions, "All America is my fatherland."

His decision to disobey won him the undying hatred of the Buenos Aires politicians. The storm of abuse that broke when his refusal became known in the city passed all belief. The hero of Maipú was the victim of the most violent insults. He was a traitor, he had turned his back on his country, he was threatened with court martial should he ever return. The Chileans had bribed him with five hundred thousand pesos, he had robbed the treasury of Chile, he was no better than a low thief. San Martín stood his ground, and commented in his reserved way to his friend, O'Higgins: "It seems that revolutions open a vast field of malevolence and that it is chiefly directed against those who have the misfortune to command."

116

The loyal Irishman stood by him, assuring him that any man with good sense would realize the sincerity of his motives. "It is only a passing storm, keep a stiff upper lip," he wrote. Day after day he fought San Martín's battles, while the latter, embittered and silent, went his quiet way, busy with a thousand details of the campaign against Lima, the City of Kings.

Chapter XIV

ON TO PERU

DURING the months preceding the invasion of Peru, the idols of Santiago were Lord Cochrane and his lovely blonde wife. Never had the Chileans seen a gentleman so winning, a harder drinker, a more reckless gambler than the witty Lord Thomas. Lady Cochrane's expert horsemanship made her equally a favorite, although enthusiasm was somewhat dampened by her excessive dislike of the ubiquitous smoking of large black cigars. San Martín, fascinated by the personality of the newcomers, spent much time in their company, and plans were made in a most congenial atmosphere.

In the meantime the fleet was being organized; it consisted of eight war vessels and sixteen transports. In August, 1820, it was about ready to leave, and the task of loading the ships began. San Martín and O'Higgins were present at a secret reunion of the Lautaro Lodge in Santiago, and met at night with the Senate which entrusted San Martín with the direction of the war. His old friend Godoy Cruz had just become head of the government at Mendoza, and to him San Martín wrote, "I am going to make one last effort on behalf of America. If this, because of continued disorders and anarchy, is not successful, I shall abandon the country for my soul is in no mood to witness its ruin." His rupture with Buenos Aires filled

118

him with depression, and the storm of abuse poured on him from that quarter was a constant nervous torment.

At last dawned the morning of August 20. The fleet sailed, under the leadership of Lord Cochrane; San Martín stood on the deck of the vessel which bore his name. The harbor of Valparaiso and the surrounding hills were swarming with Chileans who had come from far and wide to speed the fleet on its way. They felt themselves a free people in what would soon be a completely free America. There was no doubt in their minds as to the outcome.

As the white sails moved and the vessels glided away, the bands on the ships played the Argentine national hymn and the spectators roared their applause. The shore echoed with *"Viva San Martín," "Viva la libertad," "Viva la patria"*; but it was with a deep bitterness that San Martín watched the sharp hills receding into the distance. He was ill, he had only about four thousand of the six thousand men he had counted on to make the campaign, and his own countrymen were calling him a traitor; but they were at last on the road to Peru, and even if everything else tumbled into ruin, the cause of freedom would triumph.

The brilliant Lord Cochrane was a commander, not a follower. With excessive irritation he read his instructions from the Argentine government, which he had been ordered to open only when the fleet was on its way. "The object of the expedition is to free Peru from Spanish domination, to raise her to the rank of a free and sovereign power, and thus to complete the sublime task of establishing the independence of South America. Captain General José de San Martín is the Chief to whom the Government of the Republic has given the *entire* charge of this great enterprise." Furthermore, O'Higgins, in secret instructions, had informed San Martín that if Admiral Cochrane disobeyed his orders, he was to be supplanted by a more tractable officer. It was not to be a war of conquest, but a war for the liberation of the Peruvian people; the expeditionary force bore the title, "Liberating Army of Peru," and of the forty-five hundred men, about half were Argentinians and half Chileans.

In spite of careful preparations, it was a leap into the dark. The odds against them were tremendous. In Peru were twenty-three thousand Spanish soldiers, organized into two divisions, the Army of Peru which was to defend Lima, and the army encamped in the Sierras of Upper Peru. They had as leaders the best royalist commanders in the new world, Generals Pezuela, La Serna and Canterac. Men of enormous experience and keen military tacticians, they seemed an invincible trio.

Furthermore, it was doubtful whether the Peruvians could be sufficiently roused from their lethargy to flock to the Army of Liberation—whether it would be met by anything but indifference. Conditions in that country were vastly different from those in Chile or Argentina; Peru remained then, as always, the stronghold of Spanish loyalty. From the time when the descendant of the Incas, Tupac Amaru, had been tortured to death in the square at Lima in 1787, until 1820, Royalist power was unchallenged, in spite of some murmurings. The aborigines, the black slaves, the apathetic mestizos and the small group of aristocratic, politically all-powerful Spaniards, constituted a population which made for extreme conservatism. Because of its precious metals, Peru had always been the favorite colony of the crown. There the course of the revolution in other parts of America had been followed with apprehension, only to be succeeded by wild popular demonstrations of joy at the news of the disaster at Concharrayada, which convinced Lima that the rebels were crushed forever. Firm in their wishful thinking, victory parades marched the streets and the church bells rang at every hour of the day and night.

To General Pezuela's honor let it be recorded that he reproved the Peruvian officer who said he hated his own parents because he was born in America, and that if he knew in what part of his body American blood circulated, he would let it out. The aristocracy was consumed with hatred of the rebels. Such patriotic emotion, however, is not only to be met with in Peru. The Peruvian officer's remark is reminiscent of that of the professor's wife in our own country who said she tore up the pansy beds from her garden at the time of World War I because the seeds came from Germany.

In Lima they supposed all was well until the evening of May 4, when a postchaise drove up to the city gates with the badly shaken General Osorio, who had fled all the way from Maipú. The city was in a panic. The only hope was that any day an expedition might appear from Spain with money and men to save them. In vain they scanned the horizon at Callao, Lima's seaport; the only news that came was that Thomas Lord Cochrane had swept the existing Spanish fleet from the Pacific, and no more boats were coming from the old world. The mother country could not help.

Weeks went by. For the first time in its history, the City of Kings felt the pinch of poverty. As it was still under the Spanish monopoly, commerce was at a standstill. Travelers from the south rode in occasionally and talked of nothing but Chile's prosperity since the liberation—of the thriving harbor of Valparaiso with its ships loading wine and corn for Europe, sailing home again with manufactured goods from England. The unstable and emotional people, more highstrung than the Argentinians, were rendered hysterical by alarming rumors of the enemy's approach. Fox Warfare and the Fifth Column in the city played effective parts. Distrust of one's neighbor, suspicion of spies, terror of a future rendered horrid with rebel atrocities—all this created an atmosphere which undermined morale and increased chances of San Martín's victory.

Through his friends within the walls of Lima, the General was constantly informed by secret notes of the state of the populace. He decided to play a waiting game in the campaign. The fleet disembarked its troops at Pisco, one hundred and sixty miles from the capital. San Martín planned his approach: Cochrane, with the fleet, was to blockade the coast in a long half-circle, while he himself stretched out his army in another half-circle around Lima. As he had about four thousand men, he wished to postpone battle as long as possible and win popular sentiment over to the idea of independence from Spain.

On the day the fleet was landing the army at Pisco, Viceroy Pezuela was at the theatre in Lima listening to a play by Calderón. To his horror he heard an actor remark with great feeling, "*A cada cochino gordo le llega su San*

Martín." (Every fat pig will sooner or later meet his St. Martin.) This Spanish proverb is an allusion to the livestock fairs held in Spain on St. Martin's day. Pezuela, who was very stout, turned purple at the supposed insult and ordered the manager before him. The latter, trembling for his life, showed him the text of the play containing the line, and as the fellow was a good royalist, Pezuela finally relented and excused him.

The army was transferred to Huaura, an excellently protected place near the port of Huacho. There he had the Sierras at his back and in front the unfordable river Huaura. Keeping to his policy of winning popular sentiment to the revolution, San Martín had his spies in Lima secretly scatter pamphlets, explaining that his forces came not as enemies but friends, urging the readers to join with their brothers of Argentina and Chile. In World War II, the same technique is used, only the papers are dropped from planes and are even more effective with a terrorized population.

General Arenales, of the patriot army, was sent against guerrilla forces in the mountains in the north of Peru. At the important battle of Pasco in the heart of the Sierra, he defeated a Spanish force under General O'Reilly. This accomplished the cutting of the line of communication between Lima and the royalist fighting forces in the Sierras. European Lima was completely severed from Cuzco, the old native capital. The blockade tightened daily. Lord Cochrane captured the Spanish ship "Esmeralda" from under the guns of Callao, and saw that no ounce of food entered Lima by sea, while San Martín answered for the completion of the blockade by land.

Discontent was rife in the City of the Kings. Fifth Columnists spread the patriot propaganda from house to house in pamphlets written with a subtle knowledge of mass psychology. There was a different approach to each stratum of the population, an uncanny knowledge of what was needed to stir their discontent. Pamphlets were slipped in the hands of the negro slaves, the *Cholos* of the villages about the city walls, the Indians in the Sierras. Some were written by the white Creoles in Lima, following the models smuggled in by that keen appraiser of human nature, General San Martín.

He remarked with common-sense gypsy quaintness to an officer, "Before building a house, one has to lay the foundations." As this work progressed, a terrible epidemic of tertian fever, a very fatal type of malaria, fell on his camp. In its virulence it resembled the worst type of Spanish influenza. Everything stood still. The campaign lagged, and San Martín himself lay prostrated by the fever for several weeks. It was indeed a dark hour for him, for he had troubles enough. No financial aid at all was coming from Chile, the men in Cochrane's fleet were grumbling over the lack of pay, and the civil war that raged in Argentina had paralyzed the campaign of Güemes, the gaucho, who was barely able to hold the boundaries of Upper Peru. Early in 1821, Pezuela, the Viceroy of Peru, was deposed by a group of his officers, and General José La Serna was made Viceroy in his place. The horizon began to grow brighter, and San Martín resolved to try to end the war by an honorable peace with independence.

Negotiations were opened with La Serna, an armistice was arranged at Punchauca, Peru, on May 3, 1821, and a formal interview took place between La Serna, resplendent in a uniform crossed by the crimson band of his high office, and San Martín, who wore his uniform of the Grenadiers. The latter with his characteristic desire to avoid unnecessary bloodshed, argued earnestly for peace. He knew La Serna's liberal sympathies and that he had supported the ill-fated liberal constitution in Spain, so he pleaded eloquently for the brotherhood of all liberals throughout the world. Let the liberals of Spain and America understand one another, he continued. It was no longer possible for the Spanish colonial system to exist. The war might be prolonged, but the result could not be in doubt where millions of men desire their independence, "who would serve humanity better if in place of ephemeral advantages, they could offer emporiums to commerce, fruitful and peaceful permanent relations between men of the same race, who speak the same language and have, one and all, the intense desire to be free. If your Excellency will agree to the cessation of this useless struggle, and unite your banners with ours to proclaim the independence of Peru, the two armies will embrace one another."

This last remark was probably true. The bitterness lay in the small groups on each side, the Spanish aristocrats in the royalist army and the wealthy Creoles among the patriots. Among the soldiers such hatred as existed was an artificial feeling promoted by incessant propaganda. The terms proposed by San Martín were that the Viceroy appoint a regent to govern an independent Peru until such time as Spain decided on a prince of the royal house to occupy the throne of the new nation.

At this crisis, San Martín's attitude to government was

most important. He felt the only suitable type of government for the Spanish colonies in the new world was a liberal constitutional monarchy on the model of England's. This opinion was the result of years of thoughtful deliberation. Always a believer in democracy—although disillusioned by mob power and its possibilities for savagery—he had advocated a republican form of government at the time of his return to Argentina. The chaotic condition of that country when he was making superhuman efforts to organize his Andean expedition disgusted him; the almost insurmountable obstacles which politics laid in the way of the Peruvian expedition, and which were only vanquished by his complete break with the government, made him feel that new nations were too immature to govern themselves as republics, and that the result of such governments would only be endless revolutions. He convinced himself that a constitutional monarchy, with the respect inspired by the person of the king, would be a guarantee of peace until training in government rendered the people more responsible. Republics were unknown quantities in the early nineteenth century, and to most European-trained men republicanism meant only the disorders of the French revolution. San Martín, nevertheless, looked on himself as a "republican." He wrote to his friend, Guido, in 1828, "You have been five years in my company; you, more than anyone, must have known my hatred of luxury and class distinctions; in short, of everything that is known as aristocracy. By inclination and principle, I love the republican government and nobody is a more thorough one than I am."

San Martín, therefore, made the proposition of a constitutional monarchy for an independent Peru, and La

126

Serna, who was sympathetic, was deeply moved. At banquet that followed, the Viceroy rose and offered a toast:

"To the success of the meeting of Punchauca." And San Martín replied, "To the prosperity of Spain and America; to brotherhood between Europeans and Americans."

Unfortunately the peace talks came to nothing. The Viceroy and his suite rode into Lima and consulted with the higher officers of the army. Extreme reactionaries violently opposed the acceptance of the propositions. Hostilities were resumed.

The journal of Captain Basil Hall, an Englishman stationed in Lima at the time, describes vividly the condition of the city. The armistice had just fallen through and Captain Hall went up to the palace to call on the Viceroy.

The palace had a good deal the air of a native court in India; exhibiting the same intermixture of meanness and magnificence of style, which, while it displays the wealth and labor it has cost, betrays, at the same time, the want of taste and judgment in the design. There was no keeping amongst the parts; so that the shabby and the gorgeous were blended, and one was never sure that anything pleasing would not be found contiguous to something offensive. The entrance was by a dirty court, like that of a stableyard, communicating with a staircase, on the steps of which the soldiers of the guard, in ragged shabby uniforms, were lounging about, smoking their cigars at their ease, and making way for no one. A long and narrow set of winding passages brought us to a suite of waiting rooms, filled with many weary supplicants, amongst whom the etiquette of precedence was not forgotten, the poorest and most hopeless being left in the outer apartments. In the room adjoining the audience chamber, we saw only the priesthood and the military; for, in these turbulent seasons, the value of a sword is estimated, at least at its due weight. Our interview,

127

being merely ceremonial, was short, and led to nothing worth relating.

Such was the court of the Viceroy of the City of Kings; in its intermingling of the magnificent and the sordid, gold uniforms and filth, it was an excellent reflection of the decadence of Spanish glory.

The industrious Englishman next went on board a schooner in the harbor of Callao to pay a visit to General San Martín. He writes:

There was little, at first sight, in his appearance to engage the attention; but when he rose up and began to speak, his superiority was apparent. He received us in very homely style, on the deck of his vessel, dressed in a large surtout coat, and a large fur cap, and seated at a table made of a few loose planks laid along the top of some extra casks. . . . He is thoroughly well bred, and unaffectedly simple in his manners; exceedingly cordial and engaging and possessed evidently of great kindliness of disposition; in short, I have never seen any person, the enchantment of whose address was more irresistible.

He explained to Captain Hall why his campaign in Peru had been a waiting game. Due to its geographical situation, the country had awakened from its apathy long after Chile and Argentina, which were in direct communication with North America and Europe. Even Colombia and Mexico were more open to the influx of liberal thought; in Peru a hostile people had to be educated to the idea of independence.

"The contest in Peru," he said, "was not of an ordinary description—not a war of conquest and glory, but entirely of opinion; it was a war of new and liberal principles against prejudice, bigotry, and tyranny. People ask why I don't march to Lima at once; so

GAUCHOS OF TUCUMAN

I might, and instantly would, were it suitable to my views—which it is not. I do not want military renown—I have no ambition to be the conqueror of Peru. I want solely to liberate the country from oppression. Of what use would Lima be to me, if the inhabitants were hostile in political sentiment? How could the cause of independence be advanced by my holding Lima, or even the whole country, in military possession? Far different are my views. I wish to have all men thinking with me, and do not choose to advance a step beyond the gradual march of public opinion; the capital being now ripe for declaring its sentiments, I shall give them the opportunity of doing so in safety. . . . Public opinion is an engine newly introduced into this country; the Spaniards, incapable of directing it, have prohibited its use; but they shall now experience its strength and importance."

This was extremely advanced thinking for the times, especially for South America, and it is no wonder that the officers were sceptical. But suddenly the bloodless campaign began to show results. In Lima the people muttered against Spain and were miserably unhappy. The Fifth Columnists were everywhere, distributing circulars in favor of the patriots. As far back as December, 1820, there had been found fastened on the walls of the cathedral a placard signed by Colonel Las Heras, urging the people to pray to God for the swift coming of San Martín. By land and sea the pressure of the blockade was unrelenting; the best portion of the scanty food supply in Lima was reserved for the army. San Martín played his chess game with patient intelligence. When some citizens in Lima who were friendly to him asked that provisions for the non-combatants and sick soldiers be allowed to enter the city, greatly to the surprise of his staff, he consented, as "soldiers are my enemies only on the field of battle." This kindly

129

act, whispered about the streets of Lima, slightly quieted people's fears. Days of suspense dragged on until one morning the Viceroy could stand it no longer and announced he was abandoning the city. He would take refuge in the Castle of Callao, and those who wished could follow him.

The wildest excitement swept over Lima, and the people's one idea was to rush madly away. Ricardo Rojas has described the scene in his *Saint of the Sword*:

The houses resounded with wailing and prayers. There rolled through the streets wagons and mules laden with the household effects of the fugitives. In the midst of the panic, the rumor spread that the slaves were about to rise and massacre the whites; that the hostile Indians outside the walls were about to burst into the city to burn and sack it. In the imagination of the Royalist families, San Martín figured as a demon of destruction.

What government remained was entrusted by the Viceroy to a very old and greatly respected Creole, the Marquis de Montemira. A delegation from the Cabildo waited on San Martín to ask him to enter at once in order to protect the city. He replied, "I do not wish to enter as a conqueror and I shall not go unless invited by the people."

On July 12, 1821, the City of the Kings surrendered. That day it was shaken by a violent earthquake, which old Spaniards said was a sign of divine wrath. That day saw also the entrance of San Martín, who rode through the chief gate of the city without any pomp, attended by only a single aide. As he made his way through the hushed gray streets, awed groups of Indians, huddled together, watched him. The Spaniards were hiding in their houses, but from the overhanging lacelike wooden balconies, many a fright-

130

ened and curious Limeño was scrutinizing the face of the conqueror.

He did not allow his troops to enter until an efficient police was established for he well knew that the soldiers' minds were full of the plunder to be had for the taking in wealthy Lima, and it required a strong hand to hold them in check. Confidence was thus restored at once, and the string of loaded mules soon came winding into the city again, bringing back the household treasures, while the relieved people once more went about their business under a new master.

The blacks were jubilant. One of San Martín's proclamations had declared that every person born after July 15 of that year was free, and that every slave who voluntarily enlisted in his army became a free citizen. This continuation of the policy he followed in the Army of the Andes was a death blow to the system of slavery in South America where it had never before been challenged.

The General, on his first day in Lima, called on old Marquis de Montemira in the palace which three centuries before Pizarro had constructed on the plaza so he could sit in his window and watch the bullfights. Rumor had spread quickly, and a frantic, enthusiastic mob, happy at the prospect of a new master and an abundance of food, clattered behind his horse and, shouting their *vivas*, pressed up the grand stairs behind him. When he paused in the large sala, he was completely surrounded with supplicants; the women almost mobbed him with expressions of gratitude. Lima had turned on the Goths and was wooing the conqueror for favors. Captain Hall relates that he saw five ladies trying to clasp San Martín's knees at once; "as this could not be managed, two of them fastened themselves around his neck, and all five clamored so loudly to gain his attention, and weighed so heavily upon him, that he had some difficulty in supporting himself."

A gloomy young friar pressed through the crowd to praise the General for his unostentatious entry and to hope that it foreshadowed a peaceful Christian rule. He was answered in the tactful way in which San Martín managed to adapt himself to the mood of every one with whom he came in contact. The friar's grave face was transformed with enthusiasm; suddenly he clapped his hands and shouted, *"Viva nuestro General!"*

"Say not so," came the reply. "Join me in the cry of 'Viva la Independencia.'"

He was interrupted by a widow whose son had been killed by the Viceroy. "Señor," she sobbed, "if you had entered Lima in May it would not have happened."

San Martín was very much affected. For all his formal, rather trite remarks and the stiff manner which his reserve made him adopt on public occasions, his feeling of responsibility for those under his charge was so acute that he was tortured by it. He leaned forward, took the tiny old woman in his arms: "He died for his country," he said. "You know, I envy him."

The Cabildo then called upon him. Utterly exhausted as he was, he had something kind and appropriate to say to every visitor, and every one left his presence in a satisfied mood. The period of grueling anxiety was allayed and the results completely justified his hours of careful planning. Even the break with his beloved Argentina and the slanders of his enemies seemed less tormenting as he felt he had made the only decision that could have given victory.

On July 28, the independence of Peru was proclaimed in the Plaza of Lima. A huge stage was erected on which was displayed for the first time the independent flag. The bells of the churches rang out in unison, cannon discharged salutes and as San Martín, on the platform, acknowledged the shouts of the crowds, silver medals were scattered among them in commemoration of Independence Day. Lima's three hundred years of Spanish Empire had vanished away like summer haze from her purple Sierras. "I sometimes thought," writes good Captain Hall after witnessing San Martín receiving the wild adulation of the crowds, "there might be detected in his face a momentary expression of impatience or contempt of himself for engaging in such mummery; but, if it were really so, he speedily resumed his wonted look of attention, and of good will to all around him."

The hardest part of the way still lay ahead, and he knew it. How interpret liberty to a volatile, pleasure-loving people who had only known imposed restraint. In his address to the Peruvians published at this time, he warns them that liberty must come slowly. The danger of giving too much and too sudden freedom had become an *idée fixe*.

Every civilized people is in a state to be free; but the degree of freedom, which a country can enjoy, ought to bear an exact proportion to the measure of its civilization; if the first exceed the last, no power can save them from anarchy; and if the reverse happen, namely, that the degree of civilization goes beyond the amount of freedom which the people possess, oppression is the consequence. If all Europe were suddenly to be put in possession of the liberty of England [San Martín always admired England far above all foreign countries], the greater part would present a complete chaos of anarchy; and if, instead of their present constitution, the English were to be subjected to the charter of Louis XVIII, they would consider themselves enslaved. It is right that the governments of South America be free; but it is necessary that they should be so in the proportion stated; the greatest triumph of our enemies would be to see us depart from that measure.

These principles were the wellsprings of his policy in Peru. Conspiracy, intrigue and danger were everywhere about him in spite of his apparent glamorous popularity. He realized perfectly that popularity meant exactly nothing and might blow away over night. Over twelve thousand royalist troops still stalked the mountains of Upper Peru; Callao, with its great fortress, remained untaken. A firm government was of first importance, and in a proclamation dated August 3, 1821, he set forth the outline of the new administration, vesting the supreme military and civil authority of the former viceroyalty of Peru in himself as Protector only so long as the country remained in a disorderly condition; after that the Peruvians were by a plebiscite to choose any government that pleased them. Three secretaries were to assist him: Juan García del Rio, Hipólito Unanue, and the brilliant Bernardo Monteagudo of sinister memory, who was made Secretary of War and the Navy.

He was greatly worried by the decision to make himself Protector, a position into which he was apparently forced by pressure from the Lautaro Lodge. He wrote to Bernado O'Higgins, "The Friends [the Lodge] have compelled

me peremptorily to put myself in charge of this government; I have had to make the sacrifice since I realize if it
were otherwise the country would be involved in anarchy.
I hope my stay here will not be more than a year, because
you, who know my sentiments, realize that my only wish
is to live quietly and withdraw to tranquility in private
life." To have a small farm in Mendoza, to spend his days
among its simple and sincere people meant more to him
than all the pomp of Peru.

Chapter XV

DARK DAYS IN LIMA

SAN MARTÍN was convinced that the enthusiasm for independence in Lima was purely emotional and transient; and to instill a deeper understanding of his vision and to create permanent co-operation he organized the Order of the Sun. Of all countries on the South American continent, Peru's population was least fitted for popular government, and he hoped through this new order to transform their sense of aristocratic tradition into pride in the achievement of their independence. The Order was to be a group of distinguished patriots and deserving men.

The Order was instituted with impressive ceremony in the great audience hall of the Viceroys of Peru. The floor was spread with rich Gobelin tapestries; through the high narrow windows, grated like those of a prison, could be seen the fountains in the courtyard cooling the orange and guava trees, while between the steeples of the Church of San Francisco towered the cloud-capped Andes. In high-backed, purple-covered chairs at one end of the hall sat San Martín and his ministers; at the other side the president of the council invested the knights with their ribbons and stars. These orders were also bestowed on several distinguished ladies; among them was one lovely person who was followed by half admiring, half sarcastic glances. She was the blonde Rosa Campusano, whose beguiling charm

136

had won over many to the patriot cause before the viceroy left the city. It was whispered that San Martín was romantically attached to her. Later, when Lima began to realize that every day would not be a fiesta with their new government, and their austere chief had lost his glamor, they derided her openly and called her *La Protectora*.

San Martín was too utterly a soldier to have either taste or aptitude for politics. Deeply conscientious, he worked constantly to improve conditions in the country. He established schools and a national library in Lima, gave complete freedom to the press, remedied local abuses, oversaw everything. General Canterac of the Spanish army up in the Sierras made a gallant attempt at this time to relieve the starving fortress of Callao, leading his ragged, half-fed men over the granite mountains down by the very walls of Lima. His officers were insistent that San Martín attack him; their march past the walls of Lima was a desperate challenge that could hardly be ignored, and the patriots could probably have made quick work of them. He, however, refused to give the order to move because of his usual aversion to unnecessary bloodshed; and he felt that the situation did not call for a battle. The news (already known to San Martín for several days) was announced at the opera house that Canterac's army was advancing by Lima. From his box, he quieted the panic-stricken citizens in his usual calm way. There were two lines of perfect defense about their city he told them; he had seen to everything, and they need only trust in him. He had made every necessary preparation for their protection.

The decision to forego battle was justified, for Callao,

137

the last important fortress in South America, surrendered without bloodshed, and its starving wrecks of humanity marched out of the city. With inadequate provisions, Canterac had been unable to relieve the situation and had retreated back to the Sierras. Three reasons had induced San Martín not to give battle: he knew Callao had provisions for only fifteen days; his own army of fifty-seven hundred men was made up chiefly of inexperienced recruits who replaced the hundreds of veterans carried off by the tertian fever epidemic; and he was already conducting secret negotiations with General La Mar, the commander of Callao, for its surrender. This bloodless victory was a magnificent achievement, but the spirit in Lima subtly poisoned loyalty. His officers grumbled at his discipline and complained that he was so little of a fighter.

Shortly before Canterac's army marched by the walls of Lima on their way to Callao, the excitable and hot-tempered Lord Cochrane sent San Martín two bills for which he demanded instant payment. One was for back pay due the officers and men of the squadron, amounting to from one hundred and twenty thousand to one hundred and thirty thousand pesos. The second bill was for approximately two hundred thousand pesos which Cochrane claimed was due him by Chile as salary and rewards for captured Spanish vessels. An extremely angry interview took place between the two leaders at the palace in Lima on August 5, 1821. San Martín explained his inability to use the funds of Peru to pay Lord Cochrane's personal account on the ground that Peru was a state absolutely independent of Chile and in no way responsible for the bill. He urged Lord Cochrane to look to

Chile for the fulfillment of the debt, and he agreed to settle the account due the men in two installments —a draft of forty thousand pesos against the state to be paid at once, the balance to be adjusted the following October. Cochrane, whose jealousy of San Martín had become an obsession since the time of the sailing of the fleet, became very insulting, according to witnesses of the interview, and shouted that he would withdraw his ships unless all the money was handed over at once. San Martín replied, "You can take your fleet where you wish and go whenever you desire; I have all that I need with a couple of brigantines."

Cochrane departed in a rage and the next day wrote him an emotional letter expressing the wish that the fifth of the month could be erased from his life, so hurt had he been by San Martín's attitude. He added, "Except for you, no man has appeared on the horizon capable of rising above the common level and appreciating with eagle-like discernment the scope of the political horizon. But if you trust to the wings of fortune, like another Icarus with wings of wax, your fall could destroy the liberty of Peru and involve all America in anarchy, civil war and despotism."

To this thinly-veiled sneer at San Martín's personal ambition, the latter replied,

I know that one cannot fly with wings of wax; I see clearly the path that I must take; and I confess that however great the advantages gained up to now, there are perils which cannot be overcome without the aid of justice and good faith. No one more than I longs for the skill to conclude successfully the work that I have undertaken. Drawn by the command of events to occupy the government, whenever the country is free of enemies, I wish to return with honor to the simple rank of a citizen.

I am ready, milord, to receive from you whatever advice you wish to give me because perhaps the splendor that is intentionally presented before my eyes, dazzles me without my realizing it.

He did not realize the vindictiveness of Thomas Lord Cochrane. In view of the unsettled condition of the country, the government of Peru had placed all its funds for temporary safekeeping on board a Peruvian ship at Ancon. Some days after the foregoing interchange of letters, Cochrane made a raid on the ship, seized five hundred and eighty-six thousand pesos, of which a hundred and fifty-three thousand were the government's, the rest belonging to private citizens. He then sailed to Valparaiso with the money. The "metallic milord," as San Martín nicknamed him, became his violent detractor and reviled him in his *Memoirs*, which were widely circulated among English-speaking people. Cochrane later betook himself to Brazil and kept up for some years his career of romantic and mercenary adventure.

Apparently the Cochrane incident had a most disastrous effect on San Martín's nervously sensitive personality. If he had felt secure in the confidence of the people or even in that of his army, it would not have had such a deep emotional effect. It came as a climax to disaster, at a time when he knew that his refusal to give battle to Canterac had irritated his men, when Lima was murmuring about his austere disciplinary regulations, and when, worst of all, his own officers had entered into a conspiracy against him, of which he had been secretly informed. No one will ever know what was passing in his mind. His mission was fail-

140

ing and, combined with a certain physical indolence that overcame him after periods of great activity, was a profound spiritual depression amounting to an acute melancholia. In January, 1822, he delegated the government of Peru to Torre Tagle, while the executive duties were given to his minister, Bernardo Monteagudo, a curious, brilliant, but unpleasant personality, who soon made himself cordially disliked. San Martín then retired to his country place in Magdalena.

At La Magdalena he lived quietly, overseeing the government, but taking no active part. Few saw him. Gilbert Mathison, a British traveler, writes of a bullfight given by the Protector for the entertainment of the country folk. The farmers rode in with their wives and daughters, the women in round black hats and ponchos, seated on their high-peaked, silver-mounted saddles; the men heavily armed with pistols and blunderbusses, sabres and knives, as if they were about to march into battle. "The bulls were turned loose into the avenue adjoining the Protector's house, and attacked by men both on foot and horseback, whose dexterity in evading the fury of the animals, and whose violent defense, excited extraordinary interest and admiration among the bystanders."

"It seemed to me," writes Mathison, "like a revival of the feudal times when, even in England, a similar festival would have been attended in a somewhat similar manner. But here were no retainers of warlike barons; all were free and independent yeomenry—free and independent at least, in their own estimation; and 'Viva la Libertad,' 'Viva la Patria!' was the general cry."

Shortly after this San Martín decided to prohibit all

bullfighting; the proceeds of the last three fights were devoted to the building of a new battleship of sixty guns. Lima, like Madrid, was a place where bullfights had been the rage, and the citizens were infuriated by this sudden abolition of their favorite sport.

Monteagudo was a very ambitious, very well-educated politician of obscure antecedents. Some called him a *zambo*, the name given to the children of the union of Indians and negroes. This was probably not true, but it was believed in Lima. In the Buenos Aires days he had associated himself with San Martín and the latter was attracted by his restless and extraordinary mental powers. So neurotic in his private life that he might be called psychopathic, he was singularly unfitted for an executive position. He proved to be a tactless martinet, interfering with the private habits of the citizens to a ridiculous extent in order to assert his authority. Lima was proud of its religious ceremonies, but devoted itself principally to its amusements. Monteagudo irritated the citizens in a hundred ways. Not only were the church bells forbidden to be tolled, and the number of regular masses limited, but entertainments were rigidly curtailed, and even cockfights were forbidden. Many of these regulations have been explained on the theory that Monteagudo was a sadist who, because of his early sufferings at the hands of Spaniards, loved to inflict punishment on all who opposed him. San Martín was listless and ill, Monteagudo rapidly came to be detested, and gay Lima writhed in the grip of disagreeable rules, and bitterly regretted the good old days of the Viceroys.

The climax came towards the end of 1821, with the

wholesale banishment of the Spanish citizens. A decree was issued by Bernardo Monteagudo, as head of the executive administration, ordering every unmarried Spaniard to forfeit half his property and to leave the country; a few months later his decree was extended to married men, and later not only one-half the property of Spaniards was confiscated, but all of it.

It was true that the old Spanish families had proved to be an unassimilable group. They conspired constantly in spite of repeated warnings and spread endless, abusive tales about the new government. Their paid spies were everywhere, and constant efforts were made to bribe soldiers. In 1837 San Martín defended himself in a letter to General Miller, saying that on entering Lima he had promised to respect the persons and property of the Spanish residents only so long as they remained neutral and took no more part in the war. Furthermore, he issued a decree asking that all insults to them be reported to him in order that appropriate punishment could be inflicted. While the lower clergy sympathized with the patriots, the majority of the higher clergy remained loyal to Spain. The Archbishop of Charcas, the bishops of Trujillo, Cuzco, Arequipa, Huamanga, and especially the aged Archbishop of Lima, Monseñor Meras, made no secret of their hope that Peru would soon return to the mother country. All in all, the Spanish residents offered an impossible situation.

The manner in which the sentence of banishment was executed was inexcusable. At three o'clock one morning the first group of Spanish residents were torn out of their beds, and without being allowed to take a change of clothing, were dragged from their families and marched on foot to

Callao. The old and sick, strapped behind soldiers, were carried on horseback. At Callao they were shoved on a small and very old merchant ship called—appropriately—"Monteagudo" where, herded together in an indescribable condition without food or drink, they were sent into perpetual exile. The eighty-year old Archbishop was among them.

The banishment made a terrible impression. Gilbert Mathison, an unprejudiced witness who described the harrowing scene, has this entry for May 4:

> On my return to Lima, I found the road between the port and city thronged with carriages, persons on horseback and pedestrians; and, on entering the city, it is impossible to describe the sensation everywhere created by this violent public measure; the whole body of inhabitants seemed to be absorbed in grief, and terror alone prevented the open expression of their dissatisfaction and indignant feeling. Many having formerly shared the prosperous fortunes of the Spaniards, were now the sharers of their ruin, and by one act reduced to a state of absolute want and beggary.

Let it be said to San Martín's credit that he himself never touched a penny of the money nor an acre of land belonging to the Spanish residents, although he did award the property to his officers and friends. It was a desperate time. In the north, Bolívar had been fighting his War to the Death, after concluding a proclamation with these words, "Spaniards and Canary Islanders! Reckon on death, even if you are neutral, unless you work actively for the liberty of America. Americans! Count on life, even if you are culpable." Compared to the massacre, by Bolívar's orders, of over eight hundred of unarmed Spanish prisoners in Caracas, and the atrocities committed by the

144

ADMIRAL COCHRANE, SAN MARTIN'S ENEMY

butcher Boves, on the Spanish side, the expulsion of the Spanish residents of Lima seems a rather mild affair. Furthermore, Lima itself had been warned by the Spanish General Canterac that if she persisted in her obstinacy in adhering to the patriot cause, he would capture the city and deliver it to the flames as he had already done with many of the Peruvian villages which dared to oppose him.

What is difficult to understand is San Martín's apathy as he lay in Magdalena. It is a mystery that has never been explained. Was the "mysterious illness" which kept him prostrate for weeks a poison given him secretly by his enemies? Was it a complete nervous collapse; was it an overdose of opium? "Our Liberator is not the man he was," wrote the Chilean envoy to O'Higgins. Furthermore, by his harsh measures, Bernardo Monteagudo was rapidly destroying every vestige of sympathy for the patriot cause. He had his spies everywhere; he paid them well for information which was only too often manufactured. As most of the competent negro slaves had been taken for service in the army, there were none to take their places in domestic service. The citizens of Lima did their own work and gave no parties. Outside the walls of the city terrible disorders reigned as wandering bands of peons, robbing and murdering, fell on unfortunate travelers.

San Martín continued to express the greatest confidence in Monteagudo and would hear no complaints about him. He had made the mistake, on entering Lima, of treating the city like an army, laying down laws as a general would to unruly soldiers. His mission was to free, and then leave governmental problems to the freed people. When things went wrong, he came down on the people with repressive butcher Boves, on the Spanish side, the expulsion of the Spanish residents of Lima seems a rather mild affair. Furthermore, Lima itself had been warned by the Spanish General Canterac that if she persisted in her obstinacy in adhering to the patriot cause, he would capture the city and deliver it to the flames as he had already done with many of the Peruvian villages which dared to oppose him.

What is difficult to understand is San Martín's apathy as he lay in Magdalena. It is a mystery that has never been explained. Was the "mysterious illness" which kept him prostrate for weeks a poison given him secretly by his enemies? Was it a complete nervous collapse; was it an overdose of opium? "Our Liberator is not the man he was," wrote the Chilean envoy to O'Higgins. Furthermore, by his harsh measures, Bernardo Monteagudo was rapidly destroying every vestige of sympathy for the patriot cause. He had his spies everywhere; he paid them well for information which was only too often manufactured. As most of the competent negro slaves had been taken for service in the army, there were none to take their places in domestic service. The citizens of Lima did their own work and gave no parties. Outside the walls of the city terrible disorders reigned as wandering bands of peons, robbing and murdering, fell on unfortunate travelers.

San Martín continued to express the greatest confidence in Monteagudo and would hear no complaints about him. He had made the mistake, on entering Lima, of treating the city like an army, laying down laws as a general would to unruly soldiers. His mission was to free, and then leave governmental problems to the freed people. When things went wrong, he came down on the people with repressive measures, and in Lima this attitude could not succeed. When the Lautaro Lodge forced the protectorship on him, he felt unsuited to the task; just as in Chile he had made Bernardo O'Higgins supreme dictator, so here he would have preferred to give the place to a loyal Peruvian. He was a military man, not an administrator, and because of his cautious, introvert temperament, he had a fear of giving power to an untrained people. Something was definitely wrong with him at this period of his life, and some drug administered by Monteagudo may have accounted for his complete apathy. The broken, melancholy invalid hiding from responsibility, in no way resembled the gallant leader of the Army of the Andes, and the cause of his breakdown remains one of the unsolved problems of history.

His officers and men had fallen into loose ways in Peru. Weary of years of hardship, they gave themselves up to dissipation. In spite of Monteagudo's blue laws, Lima remained a sophisticated city, old in evil ways. The more wholesome pioneer spirit of younger communities was lacking; it was the enervating Capua that ruined many a hardy plainsman and sturdy soldier from Chile or the pampas. When San Martín heard that his own officers had entered into a plot to overthrow him, he would not believe it; later he conducted an inquiry, but could ascertain nothing. Afterwards in Chile, Colonel Las Heras confessed to Vicuña MacKenna that it was so, but the plot had been abandoned because the conspirators felt they could not count on the army. They feared that San Martín still held his old charm for his legions.

There was much gossip connecting him with the lovely Rosa Campusano of Lima. The historian Ricardo Palma

146

states that she was his mistress and that in his own child-hood he had known her son, who was often tormented by street urchins calling him "The Protector." Chronologic-ally, it is impossible that this could have been San Martín's child; Palma met Rosa in 1847 and saw few traces of beauty in her faded features. She was fifty and walked with a crutch; but she was very witty, and joked sometimes about her youth when she was called *La Protectora* in the streets of Lima.

As a very young girl, she had come to Lima as the mistress of a wealthy Spanish merchant; in their salon in San Marcelo Street, the prominent Spanish citizens, leav-ing their families at home, used to gather for entertain-ment. The merchant disappeared in time, and Rosa, whose unusual blonde beauty and witty repartee made her friends everywhere, was won over to the patriot cause. She was instrumental in bringing over the famous Numancia regi-ment to the American cause, and many of the officers were in love with her. It is certain that San Martín employed her as a spy and messenger between the Fifth Columnists in Lima and his army outside the walls. For this service she was awarded the Order of the Sun. It is quite possible that there was no love affair between them. He never referred to her after leaving Peru, but it is remarkable that except for his wife Remedios, she is the only woman ever to be connected with his name. Bolívar could not live without women; but San Martín had made a complete dedication of his body and spirit, sublimating everything else in life to his ideal of a free American continent, and there is really no evidence that he ever swerved from his purpose.

147

As he lay listless in his hammock in the garden of La Magdalena, a sudden realization spurred him into action. He must rouse himself, for the ideal for which he had given his best years was vanishing, fading to ashes. He must rouse himself, for there was still a way out.

Chapter XVI

THE FATEFUL INTERVIEW

SAN MARTÍN stood utterly alone, and his task was still only half completed. A web of conspiracy, intrigue and danger encircled him but nevertheless he kept doggedly to his plan. Chile complained of the large share that was hers to pay for the expeditionary force. Buenos Aires gave him no support at all, and remained alienated; Lima detested him, and the country, only half subdued, seethed with Spanish plots.

In 1820 a radical revolution had broken out at Cadiz in Spain, where a fleet of twenty-four thousand men, assembled to sail to suppress the South American rebels, had point-blank refused to embark. The mutiny spread, becoming so alarming that Ferdinand was forced to give the people a liberal constitution, and for three years Spain had a radical government which was comparatively uninterested in the revolution across the seas. Two unsuccessful missions were dispatched to Buenos Aires to see if some agreement could be reached short of absolute independence, while the nineteen thousand Spanish veterans still in Peru were left absolutely to their own devices. They were hardened, trained veterans and were determined to resist to the death.

In the north, under Bolívar and Sucre, the other half of the revolution was succeeding. With fewer than three thousand troops, Sucre had driven the Spaniards back, defeated them and with the final victory of Pichincha, freed the whole province of Quito. Bolívar organized the Department of Ecuador, comprising provinces of Quito, Cuenca and Loja, and wrote to San Martín that "the war in Colombia is ended, and my army is ready to march wherever its brothers require, especially to the country of our neighbors to the south."

The city of Guayaquil still remained a problem. The Viceroy of Peru had occupied it from 1809 to 1819, and a large faction there wished to join the new republic of Peru, while an equally large faction was eager to make the city a part of Colombia. Bolívar was naturally very unwilling to lose to Peru, so as the city rocked with the dispute between the two parties, he hurried on to Guayaquil and informed the public he had taken complete control. The terrified junta which had been governing the town fled in a Peruvian boat.

As early as January, 1822, San Martín had determined to have an interview with Bolívar in order to reach a definite understanding about the future. It was the only way out for South America, the only solution of the impasse into which Peru had fallen. "The general interests of both states, the energetic termination of the war which we are waging, and the establishment of the destiny which America is rapidly nearing, necessitates our interview, since circumstances have constituted us responsible in the highest grades for the result of this sublime enterprise." No meeting was agreed upon until June, when Bolívar wrote to San Martín offering his aid in driving the royalists from Peru. San Martín answered, accepting enthusiastically.

Shortly afterwards he set sail on his boat the "Macedonia," arriving on the morning of July 25.

Guayaquil is built on a swampy plain hardly four feet above high tide. Although it was winter, the city was excessively hot with the moist burning heat that never deserts it. On one side of the city sprawled the jungle-fringed river Guayas; at the island of Puna at the mouth of the river, the "Macedonia" anchored. An aide de camp of Bolívar came on board to welcome the Protector of Peru to "Colombian soil" in the name of the Liberator. This remarkable statement showed that Bolívar wanted no erroneous impression. It was not an auspicious introduction to the momentous interview on which so much depended.

However, to all appearances, Bolívar gave San Martín a most cordial welcome. Simón Bolívar was at that time about thirty-nine years of age, and at the climax of his brilliant career. In every way he was a contrast to the Argentine general. Unimposing in physique, small of stature, narrow chested, hollow cheeked, and with a peculiar, long upper lip, his unattractive features were redeemed by the intelligence which lit his remarkable flashing dark eyes. Excessively fond of pomp and show, he was a magnificent orator who would have made a great actor. These very theatrical qualities served him well in his career as a warrior, but the superegotist, like Napoleon, was jealously watchful of his place in the sun. He saw that his guest, the Protector of Peru, was given full military honors and a gracious reception. A fine house was placed at his disposal; crowds watched the landing and cheered wildly for the Liberator of the South. The town council called, and a delegation of ladies came to do him honor, carrying a gold laurel wreath which a charming girl, the daughter of one of Bolívar's mistresses, placed on his head. Nothing was wanting in the reception paid to the distinguished guest.

In view of Bolívar's summary grabbing of the city for himself, the flattery was perfectly empty and San Martín's distaste for the scene showed itself. Just as in Buenos Aires he had removed the crown of flowers, he quickly took it off, flushing with annoyance. "I don't deserve this demonstration," he said. "There are others more worthy of it; but I shall preserve the present because of the patriotic feeling it expresses, and it is one of the happiest days of my life." This last remark was a painful effort to be courteous. His lethargy had gone, and he was completely alert again. His uncanny skill at reading character had shown him, in his first observation of the Liberator of the North, that here was a patriot but also a megalomaniac. Co-operation would prove very difficult.

The two chiefs had three interviews, all without witnesses. The first, on July 26, lasted an hour and a half, and there followed a short one that same afternoon. On July 27 the last conference took place, from one to five in the afternoon. Although several subjects were discussed, including the question of the government of the new states, the main question for settlement was whether Bolívar would send the forces of Colombia to aid in terminating the war in Peru and in sweeping the Spaniards out of the country; whether in short, the Army of the Andes under San Martín and the Army of the North under Bolívar should offer a united front to the enemy and, by a single, planned

GENERAL VIEW OF BUENOS AIRES, 1820

campaign, victoriously conclude the war of independence. And Bolívar refused.

Years afterwards, in 1840, Captain La Fond, the French traveler, had a talk with San Martín, then in exile, on the subject of Bolívar; this interview was reproduced in La Fond's *Voyages autour du Monde*. The following was San Martín's impression of the Liberator of the North:

At first sight his personal appearance prejudiced me against him. He appeared to have much pride, which was in contrast to his habit of never looking in the face of the person he was addressing unless the latter was by far his inferior. I was able to convince myself of his want of frankness in the conferences I had with him at Guayaquil, for he never responded in a positive manner to my propositions, but always in evasive terms. . . . To touch upon another trait, his manners were distinguished and showed the good education which he had received. His language was at times somewhat rough, but it seemed to me that that was not natural to him, and that he only sought in this way to give himself a martial air. Public opinion charged him with unlimited ambition and a burning thirst for command, a reproach which he himself has completely justified. People credited him with great disinterestedness, and that justly, for he died in poverty. Bolívar was very popular with his soldiers, for he permitted them a license which military laws did not authorize; but he was much less popular with his officers, whom he often treated in a fashion that was most humiliating.

Bolívar gave a memorandum of the interview to Pérez, his general secretary, who forwarded it on July 29, 1822, to the Secretary of State of Colombia. Making his own record straight for posterity, for Bolívar never forgot his audience, he laid stress on San Martín's monarchistic beliefs. He says that the latter did not believe a democratic government could be successful in Peru, and that he favored the appointment of some European prince as ruler; to which, Bolívar stated, he replied that he would never permit any member of a foreign dynasty to rule in America. San Martín argued that not only Peru but all other South American countries were incapable of successful republican government. The low level of education and the ignorance of the mixed races would have to be overcome by generations of training, and the result would mean only civil war and anarchy without end. Only in a few cities like Caracas, Bogotá and Buenos Aires were there small groups of men fitted to govern. On this point the two chiefs were hopelessly deadlocked; it was Alexander Hamilton arguing with Jefferson. It was the clash of two theories, old as history, a problem to which every people must find its own answer.

Bolívar's memorandum also relates that neither he nor his army could go to Peru to fight without the consent of Congress, yet he made it clear that if any campaign were to be undertaken there, he and he alone was to take full charge and full responsibility. So much for Bolívar's side of the story, as dictated to the secretary, Pérez.

One month after the interview, San Martín wrote Bolívar a letter. A copy was made public by him after the death of Bolívar, who never referred to it, and probably destroyed the paper. He says the only concession at all obtainable from Bolívar was that he would send about a thousand men to Peru, to serve under special instructions, entirely independent of San Martín. The latter replied he had need of far more men. His army had been so completely decimated by sickness that he was only able to put eighty-five hundred men in fighting array, and those chiefly recruits. San Martín even offered to serve under Bolívar as second in command if only he would agree to send the full Colombian army. This also Bolívar refused.

Then the letter goes on to say, in lines revealing the sincerity of a great soul:

> Unfortunately, I am fully convinced either that you did not believe that the offer which I made to serve under your orders was sincere, or else that you felt that my presence in your army would be an impediment to your success. Permit me to say that the two reasons which you expressed to me: first, that your delicacy would not permit you to command me; and, second, that even if this difficulty were overcome, you were certain that the Congress of Colombia would not consent to your departure from that republic, do not appear plausible to me. The first reason refutes itself. In respect to the second reason, I am strongly of the opinion that the slightest suggestion from you to the Congress of Colombia would be received with unanimous approval, provided that it was concerned with the cooperation of yourself and your army in the struggle in which we are engaged.

He goes on to say: "I am convinced, however, that the prolongation of the war will cause the ruin of her people; hence it is a sacred duty of those men to whom America's destinies are confided to prevent the continuation of great evils."

In view of Bolívar's obstinate refusal to participate in the war in Peru as long as San Martín remained in the army, the latter was faced squarely with a tremendous decision. His only comment was that he would return to Peru and convene the Congress. Then . . . "I shall embark for Chile, for I am convinced that my presence is the only obstacle which prevents you from marching to Peru with your army."

On San Martín's last night at Guayaquil, Bolívar gave a magnificent banquet. Smiling, Bolívar offered a characteristic toast "to the two greatest men of South America; General San Martín and myself." San Martín rose to his feet. He knew that the power and glory of his world had vanished. Not only had the visit been a failure, but he had that day heard from the lips of Bolívar that a revolution had broken out in Lima, and that his minister Monteagudo had been deposed and was fleeing for his life. The tired, broken man, with a dignity that contrasted with Bolívar's bombast, proposed his toast, "For the speedy termination of the war, the organization of the different republics of the continent and the health of the Liberator of Colombia."

The irrevocable choice had been made. He had sacrificed himself to Bolívar's superegotism for the sake of the cause, to him so sacred, of South America's independence. His keen mind realized it was the only way, and that to resist Bolívar would mean the ruin of the cause of independence and the destruction of all that had been accomplished. Without hesitation the simple soldier had decided.

A ball was going on, given in his honor, which he attended for an hour or so with Bolívar. Then as the latter whirled about the ballroom, waltzing with the vivacious girls of Guayaquil, San Martín slipped away to the boat. "Let us go; I cannot stand this riot," said he to the aide-de-camp. He gave the sailing orders, and the "Macedonia" glided down the river and out to sea.

The sounds of music from the ball grew fainter. It was a sultry evening and the hot breeze, heavy and damp, was

sickening with the odor of wet leaves and decaying vege-
tation. San Martín paced the deck, alone with his thoughts,
and they must have been bitter. To save the Cause, dearer
to him than life, he must relinquish the helm to Bolívar
and make his exit, discarded and discredited. The second
part of his life was over and the future held only exile and
despair.

The rebellious letter that he wrote to his friend O'Higgins describes his state of mind:

"I am tired of hearing them call me a tyrant, that I wish
to make myself King, Emperor, the Devil. My health is
broken, the climate is killing me. My youth was sacrificed
to the services of Spain, my manhood to my own country.
I feel I have now the right to dispose of my old age."

Chapter XVII

RETURN TO MENDOZA

AT CALLAO the captains of the warships in the bay crowded up on board the "Macedonia," eager to hand on the momentous news to San Martín. Monteagudo had been definitely chased out of Peru and was fleeing for his life to Panama and perpetual exile. His fall had been accomplished partly by the aristocracy he had so greatly persecuted, partly by the intrigues of three men, aristocratic Riva Agüero, President of the Congress, the Marquis of Torre Tagle, in charge of the government, and Alvarado, the Mayor of Lima. "Nothing could be done to prevent it," was all that Torre Tagle would reply to San Martín's reproaches.

On September 20, 1822, San Martín appeared suddenly before the constitutional congress assembled in Lima, and presented his resignation as Protector. The astonished delegates could hardly credit their senses. Thinking his decision a whim of the moment, they elected him unanimously Generalissimo of the Army, but while he accepted the title as a courtesy in memory of services rendered, he declined to serve, declaring that his presence in Peru as commander of the forces was inconsistent with their authority. He handed back the sash that was the emblem of his office as Protector.

158

I have fulfilled the sacred promises which I made Peru; I have witnessed the assembly of its representatives; the enemy's force threatens the independence of no place that wishes to be free, and that possesses the means of being so. A numerous army, under the direction of warlike chiefs, is ready to march in a few days to put an end to the war. Nothing is left for me to do, but to offer you my sincerest thanks, and to promise, that if the liberties of the Peruvians shall ever be attacked, I shall claim the honor of accompanying them to defend their freedom like a citizen.

In spite of Riva Agüero's sneers, the Congress was still loyal. Seeing they could not dissuade him, they resolved that he should be given the title of Founder of the liberty of Peru, that his bust should be placed in the national library he founded, that a statue be erected in his honor with appropriate inscriptions and that he should be given a life pension. They still hoped against hope that everything would go on as usual.

Everything was decidedly changed, however, and events moved quickly. They soon learned that they had definitely lost their leader. Before meeting the ever faithful Tomas Guido, whom he had invited to the evening meal, San Martín, from the seclusion of his country house in Magdalena, sent his last address to the Peruvians. It has often been compared to Washington's Farewell Address.

I have witnessed the declaration of independence of the States of Chile and Peru. I hold in my hand the standard carried by Pizarro when he enslaved the Empire of the Incas, and I am no longer a public man. Ten years of revolution and war have been repaid to me with usury. My promises to the people for whom I have waged war have been fulfilled—to accomplish their independence and leave the choice of their rulers to their own will. The presence of an unfortunate soldier, however disinterested he may be, is not desirable in newly constituted states. On the other hand, I am tired of having it said that I wish to make myself King. In short, I shall always be ready to make the ultimate sacrifice for the liberty of the country, but as in the character of a simple private citizen and in no other. As for my conduct in public office, my compatriots, as is usually the case, will divide their opinions; their children will render true judgment. Peruvians, I leave you with your national representation established. If you place your entire confidence in it, count on success; if not, anarchy will destroy you. May Heaven preside over your destinies and may you reach the summit of happiness and peace.

No public speech was ever more sincere; in it were the emotions of a lifetime, the heart's blood of the great Argentinian. The country's eminent historian, Dr. Levene, wrote of the renunciation that "it forms a beautiful page in the moral history of peoples. Upon few occasions have self-denial, greatness of soul, the force and superiority of an idea as the guiding principles of a life, reached so elevated a plane." San Martín was never nobler than in the hour of renunciation.

When Colonel Guido arrived, the friends drank maté, the Paraguay tea, through the silver bombilla. Then said the General, "Have you any articles to send to your wife in Chile? There is a passenger leaving tonight who will deliver them in person."

"Who is the passenger?" asked Guido.

"I am. My horses are ready to depart to Ancon and I am embarking tonight."

Tomas Guido was overcome with emotion and begged him to stay and not leave Peru in the middle of a campaign. "How can you desert those of us who have followed you

TRAVELING POST, 1820

from Chile and the bank of the Plata! We have been through so much together."

He was inexorable. "I have thought it all out. I understand the interest of America and my own duty. I leave with a heavy heart those comrades whom I love as children, who have aided me so generously, but I cannot delay a single day. I am going! Nobody can convince me that my presence in Peru would not be more disastrous than my departure."

But Guido could not understand. He saw only that his captain was going away forever. San Martín embraced him and stalked out into the night, followed only by an aide carrying his bags. Mounting his horse he rode off into the darkness.

By the next post there arrived a letter for General Simón Bolívar, together with a war horse and a pair of pistols. The letter was from José de San Martín. "I have called together the first Congress of Peru; the day after its installation I shall leave for Chile knowing that my presence is the only obstacle which prevents you coming with your army to Peru."

Did Bolívar wince a little at the quiet sarcasm?

San Martín arrived in Valparaiso a very sick man, vomiting blood. The pension of twelve thousand pesos a year voted him by Peru had never been paid, and in Santiago he hoped to reclaim a sum of money he had given a friend for safekeeping, only to find that the latter had lost every cent in a gambling orgy. The most extravagant rumors were circulated about his wealth, so much so that a comrade who had fallen on evil days called on him and asked for the gift of a house. To cap the climax, he fell desperately ill with typhoid fever and lay prostrate for over two months, dependent on the charity of a friend in a cottage near Santiago. He wrote to Bernardo O'Higgins: "It is indeed singular, this thing which is happening to me, doubtless it will happen some day to you, my friend. They are convinced that we have robbed hand over fist. Ah! if they only knew. If they only knew the truth."

When his strength returned, he set out for Mendoza, riding a mule over the paths where only four years before he had climbed at the head of his legions. Captain Olazábal, in his memoirs, relates that he came face to face with San Martín on the road. With him rode an officer, two servants and four muleteers. His Hungarian saddle had a sheepskin thrown over it and the stirrups were lined with blue cloth. He wore a wide Ecuadorian hat and a Chilean poncho over his blue uniform. His extreme pallor and emaciation made his magnificent dark eyes more startling.

"I rushed forward," writes young Olazábal, who had always idolized him, "and I threw my arms about him, the tears running down my cheeks. The General extended his left hand over my head, and, deeply moved, could only say· 'My son, my son.' "

He rode down into Mendoza through the avenue of poplars he had planted; the good citizens crowded about him. He had returned, but how changed. Was this aging, broken man their glorious captain? He told them that he had entered Lima in triumph, that he still carried the banner of Pizarro, that America would shortly be free from the Goths—nothing more. They had always loved him without understanding him completely, so they asked no

162

questions. He was their favorite son and he had come home.

Shortly afterwards news arrived that there had been a violent change in government in Chile and that O'Higgins had fled to Peru. "Now you will enjoy tranquility," he wrote his friend, "without having each day to deal with new ingrates." And "enjoy the calm that comes from the memory of having worked for the good of the Patria."

In a short time Mendoza reasserted its restful charm. He settled down at his little farm house called *Los Barriales*, five leagues out of town, and busied himself with the care of a cornfield, a small vineyard and some horses. Old friends dropped in and cheered him. One day he asked a group of comrades to dine and to enjoy some "rare Spanish wine" he had received from Europe. To test their skill as bon vivants he replaced the labels on some Malaga wine with labels of Mendoza, and placed Spanish labels on the local products. They found the Malaga wine with its Mendoza labels "good, but not of first quality," while they raved over the "exquisite flavor" of the Mendozan wine marked "Malaga."

"You see, gentlemen," laughed their host, "you don't know a damn thing about wines because you have let yourselves be dazzled by foreign labels."

Mendoza gave him the illusion of happiness but it was not for long. The outside world broke in on his retreat, spies spread slanderous stories, and his every action was reported to his enemies in Peru and Chile. In Buenos Aires it was whispered about the streets that at any moment he might gallop in with an army and make himself dictator. No longer was there any peace for him in America.

Chapter XVIII

"THE WIFE AND FRIEND"

WORD CAME to San Martín one day that Remedios, whom he had not seen for four years, lay desperately ill in Buenos Aires; she was dying of tuberculosis that had long undermined her frail constitution. She wrote him a letter pleading with him to come while there was still time. He planned to start, delayed, and then suddenly it was too late. A letter told him she was dead. "It was the death," wrote a witness, "of a 'santa.'" To the end the poor girl had hoped that she might see him. Her last days were embittered by slanderous gossip about her husband which was whispered even in her parents' house. To the popular mind in Argentina he had become a man of mystery, a traitor busy with plans of empire. This was in 1823. The provinces had sunk into an isolated condition, each one dominated by a *caudillo* who ruled like a primitive king. Only Buenos Aires retained moderate prosperity and some semblance of order, and still kept in communication with the outside world. Outside that city the independence for which the young patriots had lived and worked seemed a sorry thing, not worth the winning.

There has been much discussion of the married life of San Martín. It is more or less shrouded with mystery.

One rumor had it that Remedios had been sent home to Buenos Aires because her fidelity was suspected and that from that time dates the hostility of the powerful Escalada family towards San Martín. It is true that the couple had seen little of each other and that Remedios was too immature mentally to be a real companion. When they had been married four months, San Martín had left for the battle of San Lorenzo. At the end of that year he had gone to Tucumán to command the army of the north. Thence he returned a very ill man, to became Governor of Cuyo Province. Remedios had married a military leader, and in spite of her extreme youth she did her best to school herself and be content. No one at Mendoza in 1815 and 1816 showed more ardor for the patriot cause; she was the first to donate her jewels, and she assisted in making the flag of the Andes. On the eve of his march, her husband decided to send her and the baby to the grandparents in Buenos Aires for greater security, and also because Remedios was beginning to fail in health. He commended her to the kind attentions of the government, and Director Pueyrredon answered, promising to extend her all courtesies. San Martín saw her next in 1817, after the victory of Chacabuco. It was then the young wife realized, from the wild homage accorded him in Buenos Aires, what it meant to be the wife of a popular hero. At that time the government granted their child an income which Remedios accepted in a gracious note referring with pride to "the honors rendered my husband." She was a delicate little creature, often ailing.

When San Martín returned to Chile during the winter of 1817, Remedios remained behind, as she was acutely ill. However, she rallied, and when he paid one of his brief visits to Buenos Aires after the battle of Maipú, he decided she was well enough to return to Mendoza. When the invasion of Peru began, she and the baby made the lonely journey for the last time over the pampas. The damp climate of the capital was far worse for her than the dry air of Mendoza and she grew steadily weaker.

When she died, the man whom the multitude had acclaimed in the viceregal palace of the City of Kings was utterly alone, without health, family or fortune. In Lima they said that the secret of his sudden resignation was that he was plotting to make himself dictator of Argentina. Had this been true, it could have been easily accomplished. For a soldier of his experience, it would have been simple enough to dash into Buenos Aires and take advantage of the existing chaos there. Were he to enter the city as a private citizen to visit his little daughter, the government threatened to arrest and court-martial him for failing to obey orders to bring his army home when he was busy with the Peruvian campaign. Since that time Argentine officialdom had branded him a traitor.

The popular journal *Republican Bee* of Lima attacked him so viciously at this time that his friend Salvador Iglesias wrote from Peru asking if he should not challenge the editor. San Martín wrote an answer to the *Bee*, one of the few times that he ever defended himself. Branding his accusers as liars, he wrote, "The name of General San Martín has received more consideration from the enemies of independence than from the many Americans from whom I have torn the chains of slavery."

If the path to Argentina was barred, the paths to Chile

166

and Peru were equally so. The latter country, a prey to political intrigues, fell into a state bordering on complete collapse. In February, 1823, the Peruvian army deposed the Congress and appointed Riva Agüero as President. The danger of the common enemy was forgotten in the bitterness of warring factions. The Congress begged Bolívar for troops. Delegation after delegation from Lima implored him to save the country from anarchy. When the government was taken over by his friend Torre Tagle, Bolívar arrived, receiving a tremendous but very temporary ovation from the people. He was named "Man of Liberty" and was entrusted with supreme military authority and the chief political command. The outlook, however, was tremendously depressing. The country was exhausted by years of battling, Riva Agüero had raised the standard of civil war in Trujillo, the Congress, reflecting the lethargy of the Peruvians, was considering an armistice with the Spaniards. Bolívar wrote to Colonel Héres, "The country is patriotic, but does not desire to serve. It is good, but apathetic; it has plenty of food and supplies, but no desire to give them."

In Chile, as we have seen, Bernado O'Higgins, less successful than his peddler father who died as Viceroy, had been forced to flee the country when revolution broke out. In Chile, San Martín's name had become a byword because of the vilifications of Carrera and Lord Cochrane. The fickle people had completely forgotten his services to the cause of independence. In Buenos Aires the nervous government kept up a constant series of attacks in the press, accusing San Martín of political plots. Letters purporting to be in his hand were forged and passed about. Anything to his discredit was eagerly believed. The hero worship of a people is a treacherous thing in any country, and its crassest abuse is reserved for a hero fallen from his pedestal.

Tomas Guido advised him not to attempt to come into the capital to fetch his daughter, a plan he had set his heart on. He recommended that one of the Mendoza neighbors go in his place, for there was a group in Buenos Aires who had sworn to have his life should he dare to show his face. Nevertheless, and whatever the risk, San Martín wished to go. When he had set his finances in order, he intended to take his child to Europe and reside in Paris. To accept an escort into Buenos Aires would, he felt, be humbling both to his dignity as soldier and loyal citizen.

Conditions in Argentina went from bad to worse. Appeals poured in to him to save the country. There was no end to guerrilla warfare and civil strife. In September, 1823, came a letter from Dr. Pedro Vidal, saying that all patriots looked to San Martín as the only hope of sensible men to put an end to anarchy. The Governor of the Province of Santa Fe wrote, "Only say the word, and I, with the whole province at my back, will be waiting to carry you in triumph to the Plaza de la Victoria."

None of·these appeals, however moving, tempted him. He said to young Colonel de Olazábal, "I shall go [to Buenos Aires] but I shall go alone, as I have crossed the Pacific, and as I am among my Mendozans. But if destiny so demands, as an answer, I shall point to my sword, the liberty of a world, the standard of Pizarro, and the flags of the enemy that wave in the Cathedral, conquered by those weapons that I do not wish to tinge with Argentine blood.

168

PORTRAIT OF DONA REMEDIOS ESCALDA, WIFE OF SAN MARTIN
Historical Museum of Buenos Aires

No! Buenos Aires is the cradle of liberty. The City of Buenos Aires will do the right thing."

In November he left his Mendoza farm and rode over the pampas into the great city that had so often turned against him. He could not remain there. His child, whom he had not seen for four years, was at the home of her grandmother, Doña Tomasa de la Quintana, who had thoroughly spoiled her. The world-weary soldier felt his future life must be dedicated to this seven-year-old daughter, to directing her education in Europe.

He wrote an affectionate farewell to his friend Colonel Federico Brandsen and left his interests in Buenos Aires in charge of an old comrade. One more task remained—the construction of a tomb for Remedios in the Recoleta, that city of the dead, unique in the new world. There, among the magnificent black and white marble vaults, and the hundreds of votive chapels that crowd each other on the narrow streets, stands a simple memorial slab, worthy of the wife of a soldier. On it is written:

Here lies REMEDIOS ESCALADA
Wife and friend of General San Martín

It was the last tribute of the lonely man to the gentle girl who had woven the Banner of the Andes, and who had given him his only child. He felt tenderness for her devotion, remorse that he had given her so little happiness.

Chapter XIX

DUST AND ASHES

O N FEBRUARY 10, 1824, on the steamer "Bayonnaes," the old soldier and his small girl of seven set sail for Europe. He felt his life's mission had failed just when it promised success; the natural inclination of his introvert nature to solitude and a retired life, an instinct rigidly repressed through a lifetime, now grew stronger each day. As the voyage lasted seventy-two days, he had time to become acquainted with little Mercedes. As a result of long residence with her doting grandmother, she had been completely spoiled and was not in the least awed by *tatita*. The General did not have the faintest idea how to manage her; to make her obey, took much patient energy. He treated her as he would a disobedient recruit and placed her "under arrest" in her cabin; then he worried because she was getting absolutely no benefit from the sea air. He would reprieve her, and the game would begin all over again.

Their landing at Havre created a huge commotion. The French police were alarmed at the arrival of this enemy of kings. His trunks were raked for subversive literature, but only a few packages of newspapers addressed to people in England were found. San Martín assured them that England was to be his destination, but the Minister of the Interior at Paris was informed of the arrival of this dangerous stranger. He wrote the Prefect at Havre to insist that San Martín depart at once, while the French Government warned the French and Spanish embassies in London to be on their guard.

When the old man and the child finally reached London they received an instant welcome from San Martín's many British friends of campaign days. In England, where enthusiasm for the South American patriots had always been high, the names of Bolívar and San Martín were like those of heroes from the pages of Plutarch. Lord Fife was one of the first to present his greetings; he had been an intimate friend of San Martín in the Peninsular War and had helped him to get out of Spain at that time. The Chilean historian Vicuña MacKenna, relates that San Martín was made much of in London, that he visited at the homes of several of the nobility and that he made a trip to Scotland where, at the request of his friend Lord Fife, the city of Banff made him an honorary citizen. His resignation as Protector of Peru had come as such a shock to London that it caused a sudden decline in Peruvian state bonds.

Then came great news from America. On August 5, 1824, General Canterac suffered a terrible defeat on the plains of Junin at the hands of Simón Bolívar, aided by the British General Miller. The "Yorktown of South America" was the battle of Ayacucho, fought by General Sucre in command of the patriot forces against the army of the Spanish Viceroy La Serna. It was a decisive defeat for La Serna, who was captured and lost two thousand men, twice the number of the American losses. His bearing dignified as ever, although his white hair was clotted with blood from a serious wound, La Serna signed a surrender of his entire army, including the twenty-three thousand royalist troops still remaining in Peru. The Spanish soldiers wishing to leave for Europe could do so, as could the officers and their families. Despite the total capitulation of the whole country, officers holding Callao for Spain refused to acknowledge the authority of the surrender and kept up resistance until there was not a dog or cat or rat left for food. Then they gave in, and the long war was over.

To the old soldier in exile it meant his dream had come true after all, and on that day, at any rate, he felt no bitterness. Sharing in the victorious battle of Ayacucho were eighty of the men whom he had trained when he had first come as a stranger to Argentina. With pride he recalled that his regiment of Grenadiers, whom he had fashioned and filled with his own stern sense of duty, had taken their part with distinguished gallantry in every combat of the war, carrying the old battle flag that they had christened at San Lorenzo. And without Chacabuco and Maipú he knew well there could have been no such happy ending.

In the winter of 1824, he and the child went to Brussels, which was noted for its excellent schools and its cheap living. In February, 1825, he wrote to O'Higgins that when his daughter had completed her education, he intended, if it were humanly possible, to return as a private citizen and pass his remaining years on the little Mendoza farm. As he had told friends when he had bought the land in 1816, he could imagine no more congenial lot than the life of a farmer. His mood varied between black depression and a sense of relief. Another letter to a friend who had crossed with him in 1812 says that as a good

Christian, who because of his age and ailments can sin no more, he thanks God who directs the destinies of politicos and warriors that he is free of temptations.

In 1827, he wrote of his financial straits to O'Higgins, who was living in exile in Peru. He had placed twenty-one thousand pesos in Government bonds of that country; he planned that the interest from these, together with the income from his Buenos Aires house, would pay for the education of his daughter. Peru had suspended payment of dividends, and in order to live even as obscurely as he did, he was compelled to sell the bonds at a loss. The Congress of Peru owed him thirty-one thousand pesos which he could not collect.

While the child Mercedes was in boarding school, he led a lonely life in utter solitude at 1422 Rue de la Franceé in Brussels. He lived in one room, walked everywhere, and in order to save money, never used a public conveyance. He knew no one in the city and passed his time in study and writing to former friends at home or to General Miller.

On fiesta days or vacations he brought the child home. He took her rearing very seriously and devoted all his attention to watching her development; the spoiled baby grew into a charming and dignified girl.

When they first settled in Brussels, he planned what he must teach her, just as years before he planned his battles. He put his ideals for her on a chart:

(1) To make her kind and gentle even to harmless insects. Sterne once said to a fly, as he opened a window for it to fly out: "Go, poor animal. The world is large enough for us two."

(2) To make her love truth and hate lies.

(3) To inspire her with a feeling of confidence and friendship towards himself, united always with a feeling of respect.

(4) To arouse in her a charity towards the poor and unfortunate.

(5) To arouse in her respect for other people's property.

(6) To accustom her to keep a secret.

(7) To inspire in her a respect towards all religions.

(8) To teach her to show kindliness towards servants, the poor and the old.

(9) To teach her to speak little and to speak accurately.

(10) To accustom her to formality at the table.

(11) To teach her to despise luxury.

On this program the old soldier raised "the insubordinate little devil" he had brought from Buenos Aires, and the result did him credit.

At home in the province of Cuyo his friends loved to gossip about him. He had wed the daughter of an English lord; he was affianced to a young lady of the house of Bourbon. All of which was woven out of nothing but Mendoza's intense local pride in its hero. Even had he desired, he would have hesitated to ask any woman to share the life of an invalid in exile, without health or prospects for the future. San Martín was never a woman's man, and was in no way dependent on their companionship. That he should marry again was not to be expected.

One day a welcome visitor knocked at his shabby lodging. It was Justo Rufino, his brother. They had not met since 1811, before José sailed for America. Justo had always been a spendthrift and had just completed a term in prison for his debts. Although he was an army colonel, his pay was never sufficient. His mother had even remarked in her will that he was more of an expense than her other boys. Juan Fermin, another brother, had been commander of the hussars of Luzón and had died in Manila in 1822. Manuel Tadeo, colonel of infantry, remained a bachelor and died in Valencia in 1851. All but José had remained in the service of Spain. The father had died in Malaga in 1796, the mother in Orense in 1813; the sister, Maria Elena, had married and lived in Madrid.

Jolly brother Justo did not cheer San Martín, who grew steadily more introspective and misanthropic. He wrote, "There is not a soul that I see or have dealings with; as a result of my experiences in the War of Independence, I have grown weary of the human race." He brooded over the sneers and slanders of his enemies, and restlessly made plans for trips he would take when Mercedes' school days were over. He would settle on the banks of the Paraná, where he had been born, and divide his time between that spot and his ever-loved Mendoza. As for Buenos Aires, Santiago and Lima: "I love those cities," he wrote to a friend, "although I have been treated like an 'Ecce Homo' and saluted with the honorable names of tyrant and thief."

Argentina continued in a state of constant disorder and civil war, just as he predicted. He wrote to Guido that something more than mere national pride was needed to maintain independence. Citizens must learn the responsibilities of independence as well as its benefits. "Through natural inclination and principles, I love a republican government; no one exceeds me in this devotion. But my private inclination has not hindered me from seeing that this kind of government is not possible of realization in America without passing through a fearful period of anarchy. This would not be so deplorable were final results to be attained, but the experience of the centuries has shown us that its consequences are the tyranny of a despot." This seems to prophesy the curse of *caudillos,* who through so many years were to wreck the new South American states.

Guido never ceased pleading with him to come home. "I thought," he wrote, "you had abandoned that stoic philosophy that drew you from the theatre of fame." Again, when war broke out between the Empire of Brazil and Argentina, an excited letter came begging San Martín to come. "I have seen in the war with Brazil a new theatre opening to the glories of General San Martín."

When this war began, San Martín did consider offering his services to his country, but because of his deep dislike of President Rivadavia of Argentina, he finally gave up the idea. He felt, however, that the triumph of the Brazilian Empire would mean only another Spain in the western hemisphere, and that the oppression accompanying such a victory would destroy all republican spirit in South America. Then when Rivadavia fell from power, and Don Vincente Lopez headed the Argentine government, he definitely made up his mind to revisit the new world and wrote to his old comrade General Miller in England to secure him passage on the "Countess of Chichester."

Embarking incognito under the name of José Matorras (the name of his mother's family), he landed in a frightful storm after a passage of seventy days. The war with Brazil had terminated just before he arrived, with the victory won by Carlos Alvear; but a new civil war, led by some of his old officers, had broken out in Buenos Aires. One of his old Grenadiers, Juan La Valle, was among the

BEGGAR ON HORSEBACK

leaders. Colonel Dorrego, Governor of the Province of Buenos Aires and leader of the Federalist Party, had been captured and shot, while the Unitario Party seized executive power. It was the same old story—senseless civil war in which all larger aims were lost sight of.

It was seventeen years since San Martín had first landed in Argentina to offer his sword in the service of America. Now poor, alone, in wretched health and suspected by his countrymen, he came to Argentina for the last time. The climax of his bitterness came when an anonymous letter, attacking him, was published on February 12, in *El Tiempo*. "General San Martín has returned to his country after five years of absence, but only after knowing that peace has been concluded with the Emperor of Brazil."

This sneering article appeared on the anniversary of the battle of Chacabuco. To quote the keen comment of Anna Schoellkopf: "His answer had been given two thousand years ago by the mouth of Scipio, when insulted by his fellow countrymen on the anniversary of one if his great battles. 'On such a day as this I saved Rome.'"

He decided not to land in Buenos Aires, but to return to Montevideo, as he had always refused to take part in any civil war. Before his ship had weighed anchor to return to Uruguay, politicians were seized with panic. They were very uneasy about this mysterious visit. All sorts of rumors were afloat, and only a very few of his friends of other days dared go down to the quay to greet him. The ever-devoted Colonel Olazábal and Alvarez Condarco, both of whom had made the campaign of the Andes, came on board with a present of fruit. The former described the visit in his *Memoirs*. General San Martín was in slippers, and was wrapped in a huge overcoat reaching to his ankles. He had grown stouter, his hair had turned white, but time had not dimmed his magnificent eyes or bowed his martial bearing.

They gave him a letter. It was one last fervid appeal from Tomas Guido to remain and save the country from anarchy. Was it for this that he and his Grenadiers had won the independence of Argentina? It seemed that their struggle had been all in vain, since for the oppression of Spain was substituted the savage murder of Americans by Americans, and complete chaos had gripped the land.

San Martín read the letter and sat there, his face in his hands; the young men watched him in silence. Should he stay? How could he, suspected and discredited, reconcile the warring factions? Then he stood up suddenly and told them his decision was made. Never would he unsheath his sword in a civil war. His remaining would only mean more bloodshed. He could not help them.

The young officers stayed four hours longer, pleading with him to change his mind. It was a harrowing scene for them all. San Martín was devoted to Olazábal and had been his best man. "Embrace me, my son," he cried, overcome with emotion. They clung, sobbing, to one another. "Who knows if we shall ever meet again," said San Martín, as they all parted with heavy hearts.

In Uruguay he was the guest of Dr. Vidal. He stayed there from the middle of February to the middle of April, and the inhabitants treated him with great hospitality. Another delegation, sent by La Valle, waited upon him in April. They asked him to take command of the army and aid in the struggle to restore order. Consistently, however, he refused to fight against his countrymen. He told Guido and O'Higgins he would return in two years if the fighting were over, and then he would end his days in Mendoza.

It seemed to him peace could be secured only by the elimination either of the Unitarios, the party seeking centralized control from the capital, or of the Federalists, the party urging strong local autonomy in the provinces. He was unwilling to be the instrument of vengeance of either party in their savage fratricidal war. To those who felt that one's country had the right to demand any sacrifice, he would reply, "One's life, one's interests, but never one's honor."

The gauntlet of dictatorship that he would not wear was taken up by Juan Manuel de Rosas, a Creole of the wild frontier and one of the bloodiest dictators of all times. Then, in the words of Ricardo Rojas, "Jose Matorras, 'the phantom of catastrophe,' returned for the last time to Europe. Thirty-three years later his ashes came home to Buenos Aires."

Chapter XX

THE HERMIT OF GRAND BOURG

SAN MARTÍN and Mercedes made Brussels their home for two years more, and then in 1831, Don José, brother Justo and Mercedes transferred themselves to Paris and rented a small place in the suburbs, as the noise of a large city rendered the old General increasingly nervous. They had scarcely enough to eat and had no prospects for the future. The pension which the Buenos Aires government had granted his child after Chacabuco had been cancelled, as had the life pension voted him by the government of Peru. His Mendoza farm had been destroyed by marauders, and all he had to live on was a very small income from his house in Buenos Aires that had been given him by the government.

In spite of their utter poverty, their days went by contentedly. In the mornings San Martín worked in his little garden; in the afternoon he went out with Mercedes to parks and museums. They knew no one in Paris, and kept entirely to themselves. Justo and Mercedes did the housekeeping while the General pored over periodicals and "merry books," his name for novels and poems, with which he tried to banish from his mind the affairs across the water.

But that he could not do. Conditions in Argentina were a constant worry to him, and he could not long fix his attention on other things. When the overseas post arrived he would pace the floor through wakeful nights, wondering if he had done the right thing. Don Vincente López wrote to regret that San Martín had not disembarked in Buenos Aires because "it would have been pleasant to have spoken of the country with its real founder." Argentina was a battleground for the forces of anarchy. The Unitarios, with their local chieftains, battled the Federalistas, and rivers of blood were shed in unbelievably savage warfare. Verification of every prophecy San Martín had made about South America's unpreparedness for self government was fulfilled.

Friends wrote constantly to express regret that he had decided to withdraw from the political arena. Bernardo O'Higgins, grown anxious and careworn in exile, sent despairing letters filled with regrets for their lost dreams of creating a gallant new world. In December, 1831, Simón Bolívar died, a broken despairing man, repudiated as a traitor by the people he had liberated. These words have been attributed to him: "America is ungovernable. Those who have served the revolution have ploughed the sea."

In March, 1832, the cholera epidemic came to Paris and San Martín and Mercedes were seized and lay ill for weeks, attended only by an inexperienced country woman. San Martín's convalescence was long, filled with moods of black depression; he was struggling with hopeless debts, and he was longing for the country he felt he was never to see again.

One morning when out for a walk he heard a familiar voice calling. It was Alejandro Aguado, an old comrade of the Regiment of Murcia, whom he had not seen in twenty years, and who, embracing him with wild enthusiasm, asked him to lunch. San Martín was not prepared for the palatial mansion into which he was ushered and the luxury that met him on all sides. The poor officer, Alejandro Aguado, had become a very wealthy banker, and, though San Martín had often heard the name, he had never connected it with his former friend.

"So you are really the famous millionaire Aguado?"

"Man," answered Aguado, "when one cannot be the liberator of half a world, one must be pardoned for being a mere banker."

The day the friends met, San Martín had been going over his accounts, and had been about to apply for charity. In fact, he said that but for the assistance of Aguado, he would have ended his days in a charity hospital, but Aguado, proud and happy to be able to do something for his friend, presented him with "Grand Bourg," a small estate facing his own chateau on the Seine. It had a many-colored dahlia garden and a hectare of land planted with fruit trees. It was San Martín's home from 1834 to 1848. A hanging bridge over the Seine rendered communications easier. "Here," writes Sarmiento, Argentina's greatest president, "through long years the simple peasants of the district saw two old foreigners in the peaceful autumn evenings leaning on the railing of the Aguado bridge, gazing at the delightful panorama; the one, celebrated with that far off mysterious fame that has left deep marks in the history of many nations, the other man known throughout all the region for the inestimable gift he had bestowed on them." There was enough to talk about. Life had

182

brought fantastic changes since José de San Martín and Alejandro Aguado mended their clothes by candlelight, and tramped the thick mud of Spanish plains to fight Emperor Napoleon.

In December, 1832, Mercedes married Mariano Balcarce, the son of General Balcarce, who had become Argentine minister to France. Bernardo O'Higgins remitted three thousand pesos most opportunely; so San Martín pulled himself out of debt and bought Mercedes a little trousseau. The match turned out to be a happy one, although it was apparently arranged by San Martín who feared that he might die and his daughter be left alone. In a letter to O'Higgins he wrote:

Five years ago I had made the decision to marry my daughter to young Balcarce—his good sense is out of all proportion to his age of twenty-four years; amiable, cultured, and diligent, he has known how to make himself beloved and respected by all who come in contact with him. It is all I have wished for to establish Mercedes' happiness. My plan was to have the union take place on my return from America, two years from now, but in view of the condition of my health I have advanced the event, realizing the state in which my daughter would be left if she should be deprived of her father. So it is that the marriage took place nine days ago. The young couple have left yesterday to embark at the port of Havre for Buenos Aires.

Mercedes, either in spite of or because of her stern military upbringing, made a success of her life by making her family ideally happy. She was an intelligent, charming girl of more disciplined nature than her mother who had always lacked maturity of personality. Mercedes was an excellent artist, a charming conversationalist. In the new family and in his enjoyment of the two little granddaughters, San Martín found consolation.

After Mercedes' marriage, he led a quiet life at Grand Bourg, cultivating American plants, practising manual arts, carrying on the humble life of an ascetic. He loved his retreat and intended to remain until it was possible to recross the ocean to revisit Mendoza. There came to visit him many children of those who had been his companions in America, among them Daniel Guido Spano, a son of Tomas Guido; a young Argentine poet, Florencio Balcarce; and a son of General Prieto, who wrote him that the youth was the tiny boy who used to sit on General San Martín's lap when he visited them in Chile. The poet Balcarce, whose brother married Mercedes, gives glimpses of San Martín. Sometimes he found him gardening, another day working at carpentering about the place. "Mercedes," he told Balcarce, "spends her life struggling with the *chiquitas* who grow daily more mischievous. Pepa understands French and English though she doesn't speak yet. Merceditas is never quiet a second." Once when this child went weeping to her grandfather, he quieted her by pinning on her dress a gold medal. It was the Medal of Bailen, conferred on him for valor when he fought Napoleon. He never asked for it again, but Mercedes put it away and it is now in the Museo San Martín in Buenos Aires.

Louis Philippe, King of France, had heard much of the old hero and wished to have San Martín presented to him; but the latter declined, saying he was no courtier and that he had come to France for silence and solitude. In 1841 his restless British friend General Miller proposed a joint

184

MARKET PLACE

trip to Constantinople, Persia, Egypt, Jerusalem, India, China, and New York; but San Martín felt actually faint at the contemplation of such activity.

In 1843, Juan Bautista Alberdi, the Argentine author, came to Paris and met him for the first time; he was impressed by San Martín's fine classical head, with the thick hair now entirely white. He spoke of his dark skin, "I thought him an Indian, as so often he had been described to me." In the Grand Bourg's sala, there hung on the wall the curved sabre he had used in his battles, and his greatest treasure, the standard of Pizarro. When he had left Peru with the title of "Founder of the Liberties," he had been awarded this banner which had belonged to Pizarro the Conqueror. As he showed it to young Alberdi, the latter realized how widely the two heroes' personalities differed—Pizarro, so cruel and self-seeking, San Martín so unselfish, so humble a follower of a great ideal. The thought came to him, "He is the conqueror of Pizarro."

One day General San Martín visited a school where Vicente Rosales, the son of a former comrade, was a pupil. He took the boy out on a school holiday, and as they walked in the Tuileries gardens, suddenly asked him, "And what do they say of me in Argentina and in Chile?" The boy stammered and turned red. "The truth, I want the truth," urged the old man.

"They say you are very rich with the treasures you brought away secretly and that you are squandering your fortune in high living."

There was a silence, the shabby General buried his face in his hands. The boy, who afterwards told the story, noted the worn clothes, the shoes full of holes, and broke down sobbing.

The years slipped by, and it went hard with Argentina. In 1829 Juan Manuel Rosas, ablest of the *caudillos*, was elected Governor of the Province of Buenos Aires "with such extraordinary powers as he might deem necessary." His was an illustrious colonial family of wealth and prominence. When he had raised livestock on his immense ranches, he had become a hero to the gauchos who looked on him as a hard master but a leader who commanded devotion. He was absolutely fearless as a fighter and horseman, an able officer, but a man of the frontier who knew no mercy to an opponent. His election by the legislature meant the triumph of the Federalists and control by an iron ruler who kept order at the point of a sword. After his first term of office, he retired to fight a victorious war against the Indians, but through an elaborate political machine, he never once relaxed his grip on Buenos Aires. He was then re-elected Governor, to serve as long as he thought advisable and the sum total of public authority was vested in him. Of course there was a plebiscite, which seems to have been as perfectly controlled as the plebiscites of Adolf Hitler. Argentina had delivered itself to one of the most pitiless tyrants in the history of the world.

Rosas was known as the Machiavelli of the Pampas. Until 1852 he ruled supreme, torturing and killing those whom his terrible band of spies, the Mazorca, delivered into his clutches. The man was undoubtedly suffering from a form of epilepsy which took the form of attacks of homicidal mania. No torture was too frightful for those who opposed him, and not only were his murdering

186

soldiers loosed on the *salvajes Unitarios,* but on anyone who happened to be about when these sudden fits of fury seized him. Thousands of innocent persons were slaughtered. Sometimes he sent wagons of his victims' skulls through the streets while their drivers shouted that here were fine peaches for sale. He liked to carry out his executions to the strains of diabolical music, and the unfortunates were dispatched with dull or short-bladed swords in order to protract the agony as long as possible. Those who could get away fled the country and spies lurked everywhere hoping to curry favor. The people of Buenos Aires, paralyzed with terror, painted the doors of their houses red, the official color of the dictator's party, wore red vests and red badges. Perfectly powerless, they became so utterly demoralized by terror that the ignorant prayed to the cruel sadist, following the example of one of his chiefs who announced that "it was right to adore God, but even more fitting to adore the 'Restorer of the Laws.'" A frequent ceremony was that called *la función del retrato,* in which Rosas' portrait was placed in a wagon drawn through the streets by men dressed as generals and women in ball dresses. It remains one of the strangest examples of mass hysteria in all history.

Sometimes he was in a whimsical mood. One day a delegation of aristocratic ladies waited on him with felicitations on having driven the *Unitarios* out of existence. He received them graciously enough but then rose and said, "Follow me, ladies, because in honor of the occasion we shall all go riding." He led the way to a patio where piles of brooms were stacked in heaps, straddled one and started off as if on a gallop, ordering the ladies each to take her broom, mount it, and follow him at breakneck speed out into the street until most of them fell exhausted. Caligula in his wildest days was no madder.

If one can admit that good can come out of evil, it can be admitted that he wrecked the power of all the *caudillo* leaders of the provinces; thus, in spite of his political beliefs, he created a government at Buenos Aires that was completely centralized and strong. The danger of a stalemate between warring provinces had come to an end, as well as the possibility that the provinces would separate and create independent principalities. Up through a bloody whirlpool Argentina gradually emerged into a nation.

All who represented her culture and her civilized ideals were dead, in hiding, or had sought refuge in Europe; and often the young men refugees would visit San Martín in his retreat. He did not entirely share their viewpoint, for while deploring the massacres, he could not look on Rosas as an unmixed curse because he felt that the unification of the nation was being accomplished. Just as defenders of the French and Russian revolutions feel that in spite of the atrocities, a transcendent ideal was born, and that no tremendous change can be effected without its attendant suffering to individuals, San Martín stressed the point that at least they were working out their future free from the manipulation of nations overseas, and he prayed that in time these excesses would pass away.

The situation in Argentina was not overlooked by foreign governments. In 1838 the French blockaded the Plata River, proceeding against Rosas' government, and San Martín, following his principle of only taking part in war against foreign aggression, wrote offering his service

188

to Argentina. Rosas, however, was a most suspicious tyrant and wrote an artful letter thanking him yet graciously advising him to remain in Europe where he could be more useful.

In 1845 came a new threat, by England and France, against Argentina. San Martín wrote again: "This is a most unjust aggression and use of force against our country by these two powers. Argentina still has an old defender of her honor and independence. Although the state of my health deprives me of this satisfaction, at least I can express these sentiments to you, as well as my certain confidence in the triumph of justice."

In his annual message to the Legislature in 1849, Rosas paid San Martín official homage, pointing out the merits that entitled him to national gratitude. San Martín continued to look on him as a man of blood and iron who had outgeneraled England and France in their designs to get a foothold in Argentina. In his will he bequeathed his sword to Rosas, not in the least because he was a dictator, but because he saw that the gaucho epileptic realized the danger of giving an inch of American soil to a foreign power. He felt that by the clever treaties made with England and Frence, to Argentina's advantage, Rosas had kept the continent American.

In 1848 San Martín wrote an important letter to General Castilla in which he briefly reviewed his military career, stating that in the ten years of public service in the new world, two principles had actuated him: (1) Never to become mixed up with the political parties which alternately dominated Buenos Aires during that period; (2) to look on all the American states into which the forces under his command penetrated, as sister states, all interested in a similar holy purpose. He went on to make an important statement about his leaving Peru.

I would have felt the most complete satisfaction if I could have put an end to the War of Independence in Peru, but my interview with General Bolívar at Guayaquil convinced me, in spite of his protests, that the only obstacle to his coming into Peru with his army was the presence of General San Martín, notwithstanding the sincerity with which I offered to place myself under his command with all the men under my command. . . . If America has any cause of gratitude towards me, it is for my withdrawal from Lima, a step that not only compromised my honor and reputation but was the more painful for me as I realized that with the united forces of Colombia, the War of Independence would have been entirely over in the year 1823; but this costly sacrifice and the equally difficult one of having to guard absolute silence (so necessary under the circumstances) concerning the motives which induced me to such a step, are efforts which you can realize and which not every one is able to appreciate.

Nothing more need be said about the Guayaquil interview. It was long considered a mystery because of San Martín's silence and his unwillingness at that time to say or do anything that might injure Bolívar's prestige with the patriots. He often said he would trust to the judgment of history. No doubt now exists that the jealous vanity of Bolívar and San Martín's own unselfish patriotism caused him to resign his future for the sake of American independence.

Chapter XXI

NIGHTFALL

IN 1848 the reign of Louis Philippe ended with revolution and the Second Republic began. San Martín was too tired and ill to appreciate the underlying meaning of the violent change as a triumph of liberalism against reaction. He saw only the disorder, the bloody street fights. Because of his anxiety over Mercedes and her children, he decided to move them to the safety of Boulogne on the sea. Old, and blind from a growing cataract, he settled in this last retreat. He could no longer see to work; his daughter read to him constantly and wrote the letters which he dictated and just managed to sign with a quavering signature. The twilight was fast settling into night for the Captain of the Andes. He took the gloomiest view of conditions in France:

The maxims of hatred infiltrated by demagogues of the working class against those who are owners; the many political parties into which the nation is divided; the uncertainty of a general war, very probable in Europe; the paralysis of industry; a million and a half, or two million workers who will be without employment next winter, and deprived of all means of existence; this future inspires a grave lack of confidence, especially in Paris, where all the inhabitants of means desire ardently that the status quo should continue, preferring the government of the military sabre to falling into the power of the Socialist parties. To continue the state of confusion and disorder in which France, as well as a large part of Europe finds itself, does not permit us to figure the consequences and result of this immense revolution; but the greatest probability now is a civil war, which will be most difficult to avoid unless the attention of the parties should be distracted by a general European War accompanied by Revolutionary propaganda, a gloomy outlook, but politicians do not care for consequences.

He remained to the end one of the old order, and he never changed his political ideas. Of socialism he could make nothing but the disorderly rule of the mob. As a blind old man in Boulogne, his beliefs were those he had held as a young officer when his friend was murdered by the rioters in Cadiz. He favored a king governing by constitutional government, held to his place by constitutional guarantees and restrictions. The recent orderliness of Great Britain with its restrictions of class and conventions was always his ideal, although he feared the system was inapplicable to the new America, where the new republics kept alternating between disorders and the dictatorships he would have so wished to avoid. Somehow the old General felt optimistic about their future; with their spirit of youth he always felt that as the generations passed, they would correct their excesses. Years went by. The attacks of his enemies in Argentina, Chile and Peru lost their violence; time tempered the slanders against him. The new generation felt a kindly benevolence towards the old hero. Chile, who for twenty years had erased his name from her history, incorporated it once more in her army records, giving him the salary of a general on active service. Peru sent him money for benefits rendered.

As is usually the case, his mental activity in later years

192

was retrospective; he loved to dwell on the past. When he was almost blind, he noted in French in a memorandum book the main dates of his life, entirely apart from their natural order, just as they flashed into his mind: "Departure from Lima, September 20, 1822. San Lorenzo, February 3, 1813. Chacabuco, February 12, 1817. Maipú, April 5, 1818. Departure from Mendoza, November 20, 1823. Departure from Buenos Aires, February 10, 1824. Landing in England, May 1, 1824. Marriage, September 12, 1812. Death of Remedios, August 12, 1823. Departure from Cadiz, September 14, 1811. Concharrayada, March 19, 1818." These were always to him the great milestones.

So his last days passed serenely in Boulogne with Mercedes and the two little grandchildren he adored. His apartment was that of a true soldier, containing an iron bed and only the most necessary furniture. On the walls hung a lithographic copy of the battle of Maipú, other prints dealing with naval episodes in Nelson's campaigns, and an old Peruvian textile. On the mantel stood a clock with a bust of Napoleon in the garb of a Roman consul.

San Martín's last will was dated at Paris, January 23, 1844. It began thus:

In the name of all powerful God, whom I recognize as Creator of the Universe, I, José de San Martín, Generalissimo of the Republic of Peru and Founder of its liberty, Captain General of Chile and Brigadier General of the Argentine Confederation, in view of the bad condition of my health, declare by means of the present testament . . . etc.

He left his whole estate to Mercedes, remarking that,

193

"Although it is true that I have had no other wish but to secure the welfare of my beloved daughter, I must acknowledge that her honorable conduct and the constant affection she has always shown me have repaid all my efforts with usury, making my old age happy."

His sister, now a widow living in Spain, was his only other relative. He directed Mercedes to pay her an annual pension of two hundred and fifty francs until her death.

When Mercedes and her husband sailed away to Buenos Aires on their honeymoon, he asked them to bring his old sabre back from Mendoza for a little grandson, should he ever have one. As the years denied him that, he wrote in his will:

The sabre that has accompanied me throughout the War of Independence of South America, shall be delivered to his Excellency, General of the Argentine Republic, don Juan Manuel de Rosas as a proof of the satisfaction which I, as an Argentine, have felt on observing the firmness with which he has sustained the honor of the Republic against the unjust pretensions of foreigners who tried to humiliate her.

To whom should he leave the standard of Pizarro, his heart's pride, his only trophy of war? He thought long over this and finally came the additional clause to the will, "It is my wish that the standard unfurled by the Spaniard Don Francisco Pizarro in the conquest of Peru be returned to that Republic." In the words of Ricardo Rojas, "All this as if he placed, before his death, the will of his generous soul on the moral work of his stupendous life."

There was little money to will away. Where were the treasures his enemies claimed were purloined from Peru, the gold he had filched from Chile? There remained only

194

a small sum for his daughter, and the jewels willed him by his friend Aguado.

He expressed one more wish. If practicable, he earnestly asked that his heart be placed in the city of Buenos Aires. After making the will, he set himself serenely to meet the future. The constant and devoted care that Mercedes took of her father prolonged his life, and the nervous crises caused by fatigue and strain were rare. With anxious interest, he watched the rise of the new democracy which he was too old-school to understand. At this time he wrote to General Pinto, a Chilean friend, "One should be under no illusions as to the future of the Old World. The real contest in the present day is purely social. In a word the struggle lies between him who has nothing and him who has. Figure out the consequences of such a principle, infiltrated in the masses by the harangues of the clubs and the reading of millions of pamphlets." He felt the coming of a world economic struggle, and he was tormented by the thought of his helplessness, blind and ill as he was.

In the winter of 1849 and in the following spring, his health grew worse; rheumatism and gastric disorders attacked him. To quiet his incessant pain he turned again to opium. He became depressed and silent. Cataracts deprived him of reading, and he relied entirely on Mercedes with whom he chatted of the past, of old days in Spain, of the colorful years of his middle life in America.

In July, 1850, he was driven to the baths of Enghien, near Paris, where he met Felix Frias, liberal publicist of the Argentine, and mortal enemy of Rosas. They spoke of their country, San Martín recalling the orchards of his never-forgotten Mendoza. The old man's homesick longing deeply moved Frias, who was impressed by the fact that his intelligence was as keen as ever. He wrote:

I saw the clearly marked good sense that was for me the unmistakable sign of a well organized mind. He spoke with enthusiasm of the abundant natural resources of Tucumán and of the other Argentine provinces; and like Rivadavia in his last days, he affirmed his faith in the future of those regions. He always recalled with appreciation the noble character and generous support encountered by him for his great Chilean campaign, and his memory preserved clear and spirited recollections of the men and events of the brilliant era of his life.

Somewhat restored by the mineral baths of Enghien, San Martín returned to Boulogne. One day he went for a carriage ride, but returned so prostrate that he had to be carried to his room. During the night of August 13, he was seized with agonizing pains and had to resort to heavy doses of opium. His heart, always so strong, was failing at last. Turning to Mercedes he managed to stammer, *"C'est l'orage qui mène au port."*

The next day he was without pain but very feverish, and on the seventeenth felt well enough to be carried into Mercedes' room. He asked that the newspapers be read to him, and that the snuff box be replenished for the use of his physician when he called. At two that afternoon came a violent paroxysm of pain about the heart. "Mercedes," cried the dying man, "this is the exhaustion of death." Turning to his son-in-law, Mariano Balcarce, he managed to stammer, "Mariano—back to my room." He fell back dead.

The hour was three in the afternoon of August 17, 1850. Around his bed sat his family, Dr. Jackson, his landlord

196

and lawyer Monsieur Gerard, and the Chilean Charge d'Affaires, Don Francisco Javier Rosales who sent to Santiago the official notification of death. He left this life, wrote Don Francisco, "with the calm of the just man."

That night two Sisters of Charity came to pray for his soul. They clasped his hands and placed the crucifix in them. On the table flickered two candles, the only light in the shabby room, where lay at rest at last the Captain of the Andes.

Chapter XXII

SAN MARTÍN'S PLACE IN HISTORY

SOUTH AMERICA's two great liberators, San Martín and Bolívar, are often placed in contrast by the champions of each. In the city of Guayaquil stands a statue of the two men, their hands clasped in a friendship they never could have felt. The one idea they shared in common was the desire to secure liberty for the continent. With San Martín this desire was untinged with any thought of self; with Bolívar, his individual triumph was undistinguishable from the triumph of his cause.

Both men were in agreement as to the impracticability of the Federalist plan for the newly freed countries; Federalism meaning a group of provinces in each nation, with strong local governments, loosely bound to the central authority. It was at first urged strongly by some patriots as a model because of its similarity to the government of the United States after the revolution. San Martín was opposed to it from the first as being impossible for the South American people who were utterly untrained for self-government after their centuries under Spanish despotism. Furthermore, the heterogeneous character of the races, the whites, the mestizos, Indians and mulattoes would result in constant *caudillo* warfare. Bolívar came later to realize this although he did not until 1826. Then he advocated much the same kind of highly centralized republic as San Martín.

The famous plan of Bolívar for a Federal Congress of the three Americas is often cited today by Pan-American enthusiasts. The Spanish republics were to send delegates, as was Brazil, and the United States of America. Since Great Britain and Holland had colonies in the new world, they were to be represented, and Congress was to debate all important questions affecting the three Americas and their relations with other nations. The Congress actually met in 1826, with delegates from Mexico, Guatemala, Colombia and Peru; Great Britain, Holland and the United States sent observers, while Argentina and Chile refused to be involved at all. It came to nothing in spite of flowery speeches, and Bolívar's own comment was that it resembled "that mad Greek, who from a rock in mid-ocean, pretended to direct the ships sailing around him."

Both San Martín and Bolívar have been accused by their enemies of plotting to make themselves kings, but most scholars agree today that there is no basis for either accusation. Bolívar, with his sense of drama, felt that to make himself a monarch would mean a refutation of his entire past career. Such an attempt would render him ridiculous at the bar of history, and although he intended to keep political control in his hands, it was the control exercised by the power of a political chief, a kind of super-boss. San Martín's interest and talents lay in military campaigns. He had no aptitude for politics and it bewildered him. His personal ambition, so often expressed in his letters, never varied. It was to hand the pacified country over to competent governing hands and then retire to Mendoza and end his days as a contented farmer. He was always the recluse, the ascetic introvert, and he was happiest in solitude. He evidently preferred some form of centralized republic, such as the Unitarios advocated, for Argentina and Chile, but for Peru he felt that feudal conditions there required a constitutional monarchy. In December, 1821, he sent two agents to Europe on a secret mission to ask that a prince of the house of Brunswick become ruler of Peru under a constitution drawn up by Peruvian representatives. Owing to his withdrawal as Protector, however, nothing came of it.

Few public figures have been pursued with such relentless hate, and for so little reason. He had a reserve and aloofness that was rarely penetrated and a scorn of stooping to say the popular thing that would curry favor. Those most virulent in their persecution were the Carrera brothers of Chile, Admiral Cochrane and Riva Agüero of Peru. A cartoon of the period shows San Martín disguised as a tiger seizing in his claws the heads of Manuel Rodríguez, Mendizábal, Prieto, Conde, and the Carreras. The fact is that he was very far away when some of these people were executed, and in some cases he even interceded to save them.

Another caricature depicts him with a huge sword and spurs, riding on a burro, who is O'Higgins, and dragging behind him a flock of sheep which the placard announces represents the Republic of Chile. In still another cartoon he is seated on a throne disguised as a bloodstained lion, trampling corpses and extending a paw to take the imperial crown offered to him by a soldier who represents O'Higgins. The lion thanks him, saying, "I will make thee prince of the blood and thou wilt be first after the King."

This was the gratitude shown the man who planned and brilliantly executed the liberation of Argentina and Chile

200

A COUNTRY PUBLIC HOUSE AND TRAVELERS

from the stifling oppression of the Spanish crown, and who, refusing the position tendered him as ruler of Chile, successfully carried the war to Lima, citadel of old world power. His most bitter detractor, Lord Cochrane, was a prey to his jealous disappointment at having to play second fiddle in the invasion of Peru. On the other hand, many eminent Britons who knew San Martín gave him the highest praise. He was very congenial with the English, and had enthusiastic admiration for their free institutions which he feared could not be duplicated among his own people without centuries of training. Lord Macduff, the traveler Mr. Robertson, Samuel Haigh, Captain Basil Hall and, above all, his life-long comrade General Miller remained his devoted admirers through the years.

He had a bitter enemy in Riva Aguero, who came from one of Peru's oldest and most aristocratic families. From the time he first met San Martín in Lima he took a violent dislike to him and engaged in constant intrigues to undermine his authority. He it was who caused the downfall of Monteagudo which took place when San Martín left for Guayaquil. When San Martín withdrew as Protector, Riva Agüero, intensely ambitious for himself, started a revolution against the Congress and had the bad judgment to write to San Martín for support. He received a furious reply:

> Your coarse impudence in making me a proposition to employ my sword in a civil war is simply incomprehensible. You insolent scoundrel! Do you realize it has never been dipped in American blood? And you ask me this, at the same time that you enclose in your letter the *Gazette* of August 24, in which you denounce the Congress and declare it disloyal—the Congress in the forma-

201

tion of which you were supposed to haye taken the leading part. Yes, you did take a prominent part, but in order to engineer low intrigues for the election of deputies and in order to keep on discrediting through the press and its miserable followers, our allied armies and a general from whom you have received nothing but kindness; and Peru will always bear the blame for not removing from the scenes so loathsome a creature.

Naturally this letter made Riva Aguero a very dangerous enemy, but San Martín did not think of that. He only saw that there had been an unbearable insult to his honor. Riva Aguero was responsible for the vilification of his character that appeared in the *Republican Bee* and other publications. He is supposed to be the editor of the famous *Peru vonema* (*Anagrams of a Peruvian*), two volumes of memoirs and documents on the independence of Peru, in which he accuses San Martín of drunkenness, thefts and murders, comparing him to Nero and Caligula. He rants equally wildly against Bolívar, "The atrocities of Pizarro in the Conquest pale before the vision of the execrable crimes of San Martín and Bolívar."

The hysteria in Peru after the entry into Lima was so intense that the aristocracy, ruined by the revolution and infuriated by the expulsion of the Spanish residents, not only spread these tales, but actually credited them. Wartime hysteria is the same in all ages. A perusal of the newspaper on both sides in our Civil War, our Spanish War and World War I will show we need not wonder at the aristocrats of Lima.

When José de San Martín left Lima in 1822, he said in his farewell message that the sons of his contemporaries would do him justice. It was a true prophecy. Fifty years later Paz Soldan, the great historian of Peru, paid him an impassioned tribute:

> He was confident that the children of his contemporaries would give a true verdict. It is certain that many of the latter injured that hero's memory; but we, their sons, whose judgment is clear, declare before the face of the universe that San Martín is the greatest of heroes, the most virtuous of public men, the most disinterested patriot, the most humble in his greatness, the man to whom Peru, Chile, and the Argentine Provinces owe their life and political being; that San Martín injured no one; that he suffered with Christian resignation the most undeserved attacks, although retired in his humble private life; from his mouth came no revelations that would have stained the honor of another, from his pen never slipped the corrosive venom of defamation. In this he is greater than Washington or Bolívar.

From Vicuña MacKenna, Chile's most eminent historian:

> San Martín, in a purely military sense, is the first general of the New World, and unquestionably superior to Bolívar himself. He is the first American captain who has known how to organize an army in all its details, trace a fixed plan of campaign, carry it out with his soldiers as if on a map, and arrive at an appointed end by means of strategic combinations and through resources of ability and military science. San Martín wins all his battles on his pillow. He is a great organizer and executor of projects. Bolívar is the man of supreme, instantaneous inspirations, of sublime daring on the field of glory. San Martín freed half of America almost without a battle. Bolívar gave almost daily combat to the Spaniards, and, whether victor or vanquished, returned to fight hundreds and hundreds of times. San Martín is the strategist, Bolívar the warrior to the death.

What of Argentina, to whom the exile willed his heart? In 1862, the city of Buenos Aires erected his statue in the

Plaza San Martín. In 1878 the republics of Argentina, Chile and Peru joined in homage on the anniversary of his death. On May 28, 1880, the whole population of Buenos Aires gathered to do him reverence as the casket containing his body arrived from France and was deposited in the Cathedral. The Captain of the Andes had returned to his home at last.

Because of his impersonal devotion to the cause of independence, and his refusal to take any part in civil strife, he stands almost alone in history. He has the qualities of a Cincinnatus who saved his people and then returned to the farm; he has the singleness of purpose of St. Jeanne d'Arc. If he had lived longer, he would have seen the justification of his devotion in the great agricultural republic of modern Argentina, where the government is a happy combination of the political theories of Federalists and Unitarios, for which such rivers of blood had been shed. At present the tendency is more and more towards centralization. The president is elected for six years and not only is given very wide powers under the Constitution of the Argentine Federation, but he also controls the Federal District, including Buenos Aires and a fifth part of the country's population. He cannot, however, be re-elected until after a period of six years. The Congress consists of a Senate and a Chamber of Deputies. There are thirty senators, two from the capital and two from each of the fourteen provinces, chosen by their provincial legislatures. They are elected for nine years; the representatives, in the Chamber of Deputies—one hundred and fifty-eight members elected directly by the people—serve four years. The provincial governors are also elected by popular vote and are given wide powers of local management. As a form of centralized democracy, with freedom of speech, freedom of the press, freedom of worship, it would have met with the hearty approval of San Martín.

As he prophesied, the children of his contemporaries understand and have rendered true judgment. To Argentina he remains the greatest man in her history, the "Saint of the Sword" as they call him, the personification of unselfish idealism.

BIBLIOGRAPHY

MEDINA, J. T. *Biblioteca Hispano-Americana* (1493–1810). Vol. 7.

—— "Museo Mitre," *Catálogo de la Biblioteca.* Buenos Aires. 1907.

SALAS, C. J. *Bibliografía del general don José de San Martín y de la emancipación sudamericana, 1778–1910.* Buenos Aires. 1910.

ANGELL, HILDEGARDE. *Simon Bolívar.* New York: W. W. Norton & Co., Inc., 1930.

BARROS ARANA, D. *Historia General de Chile.* Vols. 8–14. Santiago. 1854.

—— *Historia General de la independencia de Chile.* Santiago. 4 Vols. 1854.

BULNES, G. *Historia de la expedición libertadora del Perú* (*1817–1822*). Santiago. 2 Vols. 1887–8.

CANDIOTI, ALBERTO. *El Cadete de Oran.* Bogota. 1940.

CARRANZA, A. P. *La junta gubernativa de 1810.* Buenos Aires. 1910.

CHAPMAN, CHARLES. *Republican Hispanic America.* New York: The Macmillan Co., 1937.

—— *Colonial Hispanic America.* New York. 1933.

COCHRANE, T. B. and BOURNE, R. F. H. *The Life of Thomas, Lord Cochrane, tenth Earl of Dundonald, G.C.B.* London. 2 Vols. 1869.

ESPEJO, G. *El paso de los Andes.* Buenos Aires. 1882.

GENERAL MILLER. *Memoirs.* London. 2 Vols. 1829.

GOENAGA, J. M. *La entrevista de Guayaquil.* Rome. 1915.

GUASTAVINO, G. E. *La voz de bronce.* Buenos Aires. 1916.

HUDSON, DAMÍEN. *Recuerdos históricos de la provincia de Cuyo.*

HUME, MARTIN. *Modern Spain (1788–1898)*. New York. 1903.

IBARGUREN, CARLOS. *Juan Manuel de Rosas*. Buenos Aires. 1938.

KIRKPATRICK, F. A. *A History of the Argentine Republic*. Cambridge: Cambridge University Press, 1931.

LARRAZÁBAL, F. *Vida y correspondencia general del Libertador Simon Bolívar*. New York. 1901.

LEVENE, RICARDO. *A History of Argentina*. Translated by William Spence Robertson. Chapel Hill: University of North Carolina Press, 1937.

——*Síntesis sobre la revolución de Mayo*. Buenos Aires. 1935.

MÁRMOL, EDUARDO L. COLOMBES. *San Martín y Bolívar*. Buenos Aires. 1940.

MANTILLA, V. F. *San Martín*. Buenos Aires. 1913.

MARTINEZ, MARIANO. *José de San Martín íntimo*.

MITRE, BARTOLOMÉ. *Historia de Belgrano*. Buenos Aires. 2 Vols. 1859.

—— *Historia de San Martín y de la emancipación sud-americana*. Buenos Aires. 3 Vols. 1887–8.

MOSES, BERNARD. *South America on the Eve of Emancipation*. New York and London. 1908.

OLAZÁBAL, MANUEL. *Episodios de la Independencia*.

OMAN, C. *A History of the Peninsular War*. Vol. 1. Oxford. 1902.

OTERO, JOSÉ PACÍFICO. *Historia del Libertador don José de San Martín*. Buenos Aires. 4 Vols. 1932.

PAZ SOLDAN, M. F. *Historia del Perú independiente*. Lima. 3 Vols. 1868–74.

PETRE, F. L. *Simon Bolivar "El Libertador."* London and New York. 1909.

PI Y MARGALL, F. and PI Y ARSUGA. *Historia de España en el siglo XIX*. Barcelona. 3 Vols.

QUESADA, E. *Las reliquias de San Martín*. Buenos Aires. 1900.

ROBERTSON, WM. S. *The Life of Miranda*. Chapel Hill. 1929.

—— *Rise of the Spanish American Republics.* New York: Appleton Press, 1930.

RODRÍGUEZ, G. F. *Historia de Alvear con la acción de Artigas en el período evolutivo de la revolución argentina de 1812 a 1816.* Vols. 1, 2. Buenos Aires. 1913.

ROJAS, RICARDO. *El Santo de la espada.* Buenos Aires. 1933.

SCHOELLKOPF, ANNA. *Don José de San Martín.* New York: Boni & Liveright, 1924.

SENCOURT, R. E. *The Spanish Crown, 1808–1931.* New York: Chas. Scribner's Sons, 1932.

SOTO HALL, M. *Monteagudo.* Buenos Aires. 1933.

VICUÑA MACKENNA. *El General José de San Martín.* Santiago. 1863.

—— *La revolución de la independencia del Perú desde 1809 a 1819.* Lima. 1860.

——*Vida del capitán general de Chile, don Bernardo O'Higgins.* Valparaiso. 1860.

VARELA, ADRIAN. *Juan Martin de Pueyrredón.* Buenos Aires. 1924.

VIDELA, RICARDO. *El general San Martín y Mendoza.* Mendoza. 1936.

VILLANUEVA, C. A. *La Monarquía en América: Bolívar y el general San Martín, etc.* Paris. 4 Vols. 1911–14.

EARLY TRAVELERS

BRACKENRIDGE, H. M. *Voyage to South America.* Baltimore. 1819.

GRAHAM, MARIA. *Journal.* London. 1824.

HAIGH, SAMUEL. *Sketches of Buenos Aires, Chile and Peru.* London. 1831.

HALL, BASIL. *Extracts from a journal written on the coasts of Chile, Peru and Mexico.* Edinburgh. 1825.

MATHISON, GILBERT F. *Narrative of a visit to Brazil, Chile, Peru.* London. 1825.

MIERS, JOHN. *Travels in Chile and La Plata.* London. 1826.

STEVENSON, W. H. *Narrative of 20 years' residence in South America.* London. 3 Vols. 1829.

VIDAL, E. P. *Buenos Aires and Montevideo.* London. 1820.

SOURCES

Archivo General de la nación. "Partes oficiales y documentos relativos a la guerra de la independencia Argentina." Buenos Aires. 4 Vols. 1900–1903.

Archivo General de la ciudad de Mendoza.

BERTLING, H., Editor. *Documentos históricos referentes al paso de los Andes.* Concepción. 1908.

CARRANZA, A. P., Editor. "Archivo General de la República Argentina." Segunda Serie. Buenos Aires. 14 Vols. 1894–99.

O'HIGGINS, B. *Epistolario de don Bernardo O'Higgins.* Vol. 1. Santiago. 1916.

RIVA AGÜERO. *Memorias y documentos para la historia de la independencia del Perú.* Paris. 2 Vols. 1858.

ROBERTSON, J. P. and ROBERTSON, W. P. *Letters on Paraguay.* London. 2 Vols. 1839.

ZUNIGA, ANTONIO R. *La Logia Lautaro y la independencia de América.* Buenos Aires: Grafico J. Estrach, 1922.

INDEX

Aguado, Alejandro, 181–182
Alberdi, Juan Bautista, 185
Aldao, 87
Alvarado, Colonel, 102, 158
Alvarez Jonte, 55
Alvarez Condarco, Major José Antonio, prepares maps for Army of Andes, 90; pleads with San Martín to remain in Argentina, 178
Alvear, Carlos de, 44, 51, 60; enemy of San Martín, 61; takes Montevideo, 67; wins victory over Brazil, 176
Añchoreña, Dr., 79
Arana, Barros, 103
Aranda, Count, 17
Arenales, General, 123
Argentina, Department of Yapeyú, 1, 2; Jesuit missions, 2; declares independence from Spain, 34, 77–78; sends army against Peru, 37, 59–67; government in 1812, 54–56; General Assembly of the United Provinces, 55; flag, 56, 93; campaign against Peru, 59–67; monarchal government proposed, 78; alliance with Chile, 108; civil war in provinces, 115; appeals to San Martín to save her from anarchy, 168; war with Empire of Brazil, 176; civil war following war with Brazil, 176–177; dictatorship of Rosas, 186–188; blockade of Plata River by French, 188; government, 204

Army of the Andes, organization and equipping of, 74–90; crosses the Andes, 93–94; leaves Mendoza, 92
Army of Peru, the, 120
Artigas, José, 36–37, 67
Ayacucho, battle of, 171

Balcarce, Florencio, 184
Balcarce, General, 102
Balcarce, Mariano, marries Mercedes San Martín, 183
Belgrano, General, 59, 60; plan for monarchal government of Argentina and Peru, 78
Beltran, Luis, 82, 83
Berney, Antonio, 14
Bolívar, Simón, 113; orders massacre of Spanish prisoners, 144; organizes Department of Ecuador, 150; takes control of Guayaquil, 150; meets San Martín at Guayaquil, 151–152, 190; San Martín's impression of, 153; refuses to join San Martín in Peruvian war, 153–154; welcomed to Peru, 167; defeats Canterac on plains of Junin, 171; death, 181; plans for Federal Congress of the Americas, 199
Bonaparte, Joseph, 25
Bonaparte, Napoleon, conquest of Spain, 25, 29, 33
Boves, 145
Brandsen, Colonel Federico, 169
Brazil, war with Argentina, 176

211

Buenos Aires, 4; colonial trade, 13; appearance in 1812, 46; Mounted Grenadiers Regiment, 46–47; Lautaro Lodge, 48–50; government in 1812, 54–56; celebrates San Martín's capture of Santiago, 97; erects memorial to San Martín, 203–204
Burgos Regiment, at Battle of Maipú, 103, 105

Cabral, Juan, saves San Martín's life, 58
Cadiz, cholera epidemic, 21–22; mob uprising, 27; mutiny of 1820, 149
Callao, surrender, 137–138, 172
Campusano, Rosa, 136–137, 146–147
Canterac, General, 120; attempts to relieve fortress of Callao, 137; defeated by Bolívar at Junin, 171
Carrera, José Miguel, 35
Castanos, Francisco Javier, 29
Castilla, General, 189
Caudillos, 59, 115
Chacabuco, battle of, 95–96
Charcas, Archbishop of, 143, 144
Charles III of Spain, 16–17, 24
Charles IV of Spain, 24
Chiclana, 54
Chile, rebellion of 1780, 14; revolt from Peru, 74; declares independence, 97; alliance with Argentina, 108
Cochrane, Lady, 118
Cochrane, Lord Thomas, 114–115, 118, 200, 201; commands fleet against Peru, 119–120; blockades Lima, 123; quarrel with San Martín, 138–140
Collisberry, Guillermo, 64
Concharrayada, battle of, 98

Condarco. *See* Alvarez Condarco
Coupigny, Marquis de, 32
Creoles, 7, 8, 13, 59; trade restrictions, 10; in Spain, 23
Cruz, Colonel Don Francisco de, 64

Del Pont, General Marco, 86–87; surrenders to San Martín, 96
Dios, Juan, cited for bravery in Army of Andalusia, 30
Dorrego, Colonel, 177

Escalada, Antonio José, 52
Escalada, Maria de los Remedios, betrothal and marriage to San Martín, 52–53. *See also* San Martín, Remedios
Elio, General, 36
Espejo, General Gerónimo, 71

Ferdinand VII, King of Spain, 67, 149
Fife, Lord, 171
France, Revolution of 1848, 191
Frias, Felix, 195

García del Rio, Juan, 23, 134
Gauchos, 62; Argentinian, in provincial civil war, 115
General Assembly of the United Provinces, 55
Gibraltar, Spain loses, 17
Godoy, Manuel, 24
Godoy Cruz, 118
"Goths," 48, 63, 65, 91, 96
Gramuset, Antonio, 14
Guarani Indians, 2, 5
Guayaquil, Bolívar takes control of, 150; meeting place of Bolívar and San Martín, 151
Güemes, Martin, 63, 64, 65; campaign in Peru, 124

213

San Martín, Juan Fermin, 3, 175
San Martín, José Francisco de,
birth, 1; parentage, 1–2; child-
hood in Argentina, 3; school days
in Spain, 16–19; joins Regiment
of Murcia, 19–21; garrisoned at
Cadiz, 21–23; in Cadiz uprising,
26–27; opinions on government,
28; second lieutenant in Regiment of Murcia, 21; cavalry captain in Regiment of Bourbon, 30;
decorated for bravery in Peninsular War, 32; lieutenant colonel
of cavalry, 32; aide-de-camp to
Marquis de Coupigny, 32; commander of regiment of Saguntum
Dragoons, 32; flees to London,
40; joins Lautaro Lodge at Cadiz,
43; returns to Argentina, 44–46;
lieutenant-colonel of Mounted
Grenadiers of Buenos Aires, 47–
48; marriage, 54; asks resignation of Buenos Aires triumvirate,
55; at battle of San Lorenzo, 57–
58; leads Mounted Grenadiers in
defense of Buenos Aires against
Spanish royalists, 57–59; life
saved by Juan Cabral, 58; commander of Argentine army in
Peru, 61–66; illnesses, 63–64, 75,
76–77, 112, 114, 145, 161, 195;
Governor of Province of Cuyo, 66,
69, 71–73; birth of daughter, 80;
as chess player, 85; rumored to
be Spanish spy, 85; "fox warfare," 86–88; organizes the Army
of the Andes, 74–90; battle of
Chacabuco, 95–96; captures Santiago, 96; appointed brigadier
general, 97; declines election as
Director of Chile, 97; wins battle of Maipú, 101–106; pro-
poses cessation of war with Peru,
107; return to Buenos Aires to
secure financial aid for invasion
of Peru, 108–109; offers resignation as chief of Army of Andes,
109; social life in Santiago, 110–
111; ordered to return to Buenos
Aires by Rondeau, 115–116; sails
from Valparaiso for Peru, 119;
asks La Serna for peace with
Peru, 125, 126–127; Hall's description, 128; explanation of
Peruvian campaign, 128–129;
enters Lima, 130–131; blow at
slavery in Peru, 131; Protector
of Peru, 134; organizes Order
of the Sun, 136; quarrel with
Lord Cochrane, 138–140; retires
from government of Peru, 141;
goes to La Magdalena, 141; meets
Bolívar at Guayaquil, 151–152,
190; Bolívar refuses to join him
in Peruvian war, 153–154; re-
signs as Protector of Peru, 158;
receives title of Generalissimo of
Army of Peru, 158; last address
to Peruvians, 159–160; returns to
Mendoza, 162–163; death of
wife, 164; attacked by *Republican Bee* of Lima, 166; goes to
Buenos Aires from Mendoza, 169;
sails for Europe with daughter,
170; welcomed in London, 171;
life in Brussels, 172; returns to
Argentina to offer services in Brazilian war, 176; refuses to take
part in Argentinian civil war,
178–179; in Uruguay, 178–179;
life in Paris, 180; stricken with
cholera, 181; presented "Grand
Bourg" by Aguado, 182; offers
services to Rosas in French blockade, 188–189; letter to Castilla,
189–190; views on Revolution of

215

COSIMO

COSIMO is a specialty publisher of books and publications that inspire, inform, and engage readers. Our mission is to offer unique books to niche audiences around the world.

COSIMO BOOKS publishes books and publications for innovative authors, nonprofit organizations, and businesses. **COSIMO BOOKS** specializes in bringing books back into print, publishing new books quickly and effectively, and making these publications available to readers around the world.

COSIMO CLASSICS offers a collection of distinctive titles by the great authors and thinkers throughout the ages. At **COSIMO CLASSICS** timeless works find new life as affordable books, covering a variety of subjects including: Business, Economics, History, Personal Development, Philosophy, Religion & Spirituality, and much more!

COSIMO REPORTS publishes public reports that affect your world, from global trends to the economy, and from health to geopolitics.

FOR MORE INFORMATION CONTACT US AT
INFO@COSIMOBOOKS.COM

* ✳ if you are a book lover interested in our current catalog of books

* ✳ if you represent a bookstore, book club, or anyone else interested in special discounts for bulk purchases

* ✳ if you are an author who wants to get published

* ✳ if you represent an organization or business seeking to publish books and other publications for your members, donors, or customers.

COSIMO BOOKS ARE ALWAYS
AVAILABLE AT ONLINE BOOKSTORES

VISIT COSIMOBOOKS.COM
BE INSPIRED, BE INFORMED

CPSIA information can be obtained at www.ICGtesting.com
Printed in the USA
LVOW08s1759100116

469984LV00002B/775/P

9 781605 209135